Neon Frequencies

A Biography of Krewella

Rosa Rao

ISBN: 9781779693709
Imprint: Technical Press Cin
Copyright © 2024 Rosa Rao.
All Rights Reserved.

Contents

Introduction   1
The Birth of Neon Frequencies   1

Chapter Two: Rise to Stardom   21
Signing with Krewella   21

Chapter Three: Challenges and Resilience   45
The Price of Fame   45

Chapter Four: Going Global   67
From Local to International   67

Chapter Five: Krewella's Impact   87
The Influence of Krewella   87
Chapter Five: Krewella's Impact   87

Chapter Six: Conclusion   107
The Journey of Krewella   107

Index   125

Introduction

The Birth of Neon Frequencies

The Krewella Sisters: Jahan and Yasmine

The story of Krewella begins with two extraordinary sisters, Jahan and Yasmine Yousaf, who have taken the music world by storm with their unique blend of electronic dance music and heartfelt lyrics. These two talented women have captured the hearts of millions of fans around the world, but their journey to success has been filled with ups and downs, challenges and triumphs.

Jahan and Yasmine were born and raised in Chicago, a city known for its vibrant music scene. Growing up, the sisters were exposed to a variety of musical genres, thanks to their parents' eclectic taste in music. Their father, a Pakistani immigrant, introduced them to traditional South Asian melodies, while their mother's love for rock and pop music inspired them to explore different sounds and styles.

From an early age, Jahan and Yasmine showed a keen interest in music. They both took piano lessons and participated in school choir, nurturing their passion for creating and performing music. But it wasn't until they discovered electronic dance music (EDM) that their true musical journey began.

Influenced by EDM pioneers like Deadmau5 and Skrillex, the sisters were drawn to the energy and creativity of the genre. They were inspired by how EDM brought people together on the dancefloor, creating a sense of unity and euphoria. Feeling a deep connection to the music, Jahan and Yasmine knew they had found their calling.

With a shared vision and undeniable talent, Jahan and Yasmine began experimenting with producing their own music. They spent countless hours in their makeshift home studio, honing their skills and refining their sound. Drawing inspiration from their diverse musical backgrounds, they blended elements of pop, rock, and traditional Pakistani music with high-energy EDM beats, creating a sound that was uniquely their own.

The formation of Krewella marked the next chapter in Jahan and Yasmine's musical journey. But starting a band is never easy, especially when you're just finding your footing in a competitive industry. The early days of Krewella were filled with uncertainty and countless setbacks, but the sisters never gave up.

They tirelessly promoted their music, performing at small venues and uploading their tracks to Soundcloud in the hopes of garnering attention. Their hard work and dedication paid off when their breakthrough moment finally arrived.

The Chicago music scene began to take notice of Krewella's dynamic performances and infectious sound. Their reputation as a must-see live act quickly spread, earning them a loyal local following. With each show, Jahan and Yasmine captivated audiences with their electrifying stage presence and undeniable talent, solidifying their place as rising stars in the underground music scene.

But Jahan and Yasmine had their sights set on something bigger. They knew they had the potential to make a global impact and reach audiences far beyond the Chicago scene. And with the rise of EDM in mainstream music, the timing couldn't have been more perfect.

The breakout moment for Krewella came when they caught the attention of a prominent record label. Their unique sound and captivating performances impressed the label executives, who saw the sisters' potential to bring a fresh perspective to the EDM genre. This led to Krewella signing their first major record deal, propelling them into the spotlight and paving the way for their meteoric rise to stardom.

Stay tuned as we dig deeper into Krewella's journey, exploring the challenges they faced along the way and the resilience that fueled their success. We'll uncover the impact they've made on the EDM community, the controversies they've weathered, and the milestones they've achieved. Join us on this thrilling ride as we explore the captivating story of Krewella and the enduring legacy of Neon Frequencies.

A Musical Childhood

Ah, the sweet tunes of childhood. We've all had those musical memories that transport us back to our younger days. Well, Jahan and Yasmine, the talented sisters who make up the powerhouse duo of Krewella, are no exception. Their musical journey began early on, shaped by their upbringing and the melodies that resonated through their household.

Imagine growing up in a house where music was not just a background noise but a vital part of everyday life. That's exactly the kind of environment that Jahan and Yasmine were fortunate enough to experience. Their parents, both of Pakistani descent, had a profound appreciation for music from around the world. From classical Indian ragas to Western pop hits, their ears were constantly exposed to a diverse range of sounds.

It was in this sonic wonderland that the Krewella sisters discovered their passion for music. As little girls, they were captivated by the melodies that flowed through their home. They would spend hours dancing and singing along to their favorite tracks, immersing themselves in the rhythms and beats that surrounded them.

But it wasn't just about listening to music for Jahan and Yasmine. They were determined to explore their creative potential and bring their own unique voices to the mix. Their parents recognized their budding talents and encouraged them to pursue their passion. They provided the girls with instruments and enrolled them in music lessons, giving them the tools they needed to develop their skills.

Jahan, the older of the two sisters, gravitated towards the piano. She was enchanted by the instrument's versatility and its ability to express a wide range of emotions. Yasmine, on the other hand, was drawn to the electric guitar. She loved the rebellious spirit of rock music and found solace in the raw power of the instrument.

As they honed their skills on their respective instruments, Jahan and Yasmine began experimenting with creating their own music. They would spend hours in their bedroom, strumming their guitar and tinkering with melodies on the piano. Their dedication and natural talent allowed them to quickly learn the ropes of songwriting and composition.

Their musical education extended beyond their bedroom walls. Jahan and Yasmine were fortunate to have access to a rich musical community in Chicago, where they grew up. They would attend local concerts and open mic nights, soaking up the vibrant energy of the city's music scene. These experiences exposed them to a variety of genres, from punk rock to hip-hop, further expanding their musical horizons.

But it wasn't just about listening to music or performing covers for the

Krewella sisters. They were determined to find their own voice and create something truly unique. They delved into the world of electronic music, experimenting with synthesizers, drum machines, and digital production software. This newfound fascination with electronic sounds would eventually become a defining element of their musical style.

Their musical childhood instilled in them a deep appreciation for the power of music to connect people and evoke emotions. It taught them that music is a universal language that transcends cultural boundaries. And most importantly, it nurtured their love for creating music that moves both their listeners and themselves.

So, it was no surprise when Jahan and Yasmine embarked on their musical journey together as Krewella. Their shared childhood experiences, combined with their mutual passion for music, set the stage for their explosive rise to the top of the EDM scene.

But before we delve into their meteoric rise to stardom, let's take a moment to explore the musical influences and inspirations that shaped the Krewella sound. Get ready to dive into a world of pulsating beats, pulsating energy, and a whole lot of neon frequencies.

Influences and Inspirations

The journey of Krewella is not just a tale of talent and hard work; it is also a story of the passion and influences that shaped the unique sound of the band. Jahan and Yasmine, the dynamic and spirited sisters behind Krewella, were exposed to a diverse range of musical genres and artists from a young age, which played a pivotal role in shaping their artistic vision.

1. Early musical exposure

Growing up in a musical household, Jahan and Yasmine were exposed to a vast array of genres. Their parents introduced them to classical music, Bollywood soundtracks, and traditional Indian folk songs. They were captivated by the melodies and the storytelling aspect of these genres, which would later influence their own compositions.

2. Exploration of electronic music

As they entered their teenage years, Jahan and Yasmine's musical tastes expanded to include electronic music. They were particularly drawn to the high-energy beats and the sonic landscapes created by artists such as Daft Punk, The Chemical Brothers, and Prodigy. The sheer power and raw emotion of these electronic sounds inspired them to experiment with electronic music production.

3. Fusion of genres

One of the defining features of Krewella's music is the seamless fusion of various musical genres. Influenced by their diverse backgrounds, Jahan and Yasmine effortlessly meld elements of electronic dance music (EDM), pop, rock, and even traditional Indian music. This unique blend of sounds and styles is what sets Krewella apart from other EDM artists.

4. Feminine power and rebellion

Another significant influence on Krewella's music and image is the concept of feminine power and rebellion. The sisters were inspired by strong female artists such as Madonna, Beyoncé, and Gwen Stefani, who fearlessly expressed their individuality and embrace their femininity on stage. Jahan and Yasmine wanted to create a space in EDM where women could not only be present but also thrive as performers and creators.

5. Embracing their cultural heritage

Krewella's Indian heritage has always been a source of inspiration for their music. Influenced by the vibrant sounds and rhythms of traditional Indian music, the sisters have incorporated Indian classical instruments like the sitar and tabla into their electronic compositions. This infusion of cultural elements adds a unique flavor to their music and further sets them apart from their peers.

6. EDM community and collaborations

The EDM community itself played a significant role in shaping and inspiring Krewella's music. Through collaborations with other electronic artists and DJs, such as Skrillex and Adventure Club, Krewella was able to explore new styles and experiment with different production techniques. These collaborations allowed them to push their artistic boundaries and discover new influences along the way.

7. Unique life experiences

Finally, Krewella's music is heavily influenced by their own personal experiences and journey. The highs and lows, the triumphs and struggles, all find their way into their music. This authenticity and vulnerability resonate with their fans and create a deep emotional connection.

In summary, Krewella's influences and inspirations are as diverse as their music. From classical melodies to electronic beats, from traditional Indian sounds to feminist rebellion, every element has contributed to the creation of their unique sound. It is this ambitious pursuit of blending different genres and pushing artistic boundaries that continues to captivate audiences worldwide. Through their authentic storytelling and powerful performances, Krewella has emerged as trailblazers in the EDM scene, leaving a lasting impact on both the industry and their fans.

```
                    Electronic
                      Music
                       ↑
          ↗            │            ↖
    ┌─────┐            │          ┌──────┐
    │ Pop │            │          │ Rock │
    └─────┘            │          └──────┘
       │          ┌─────────┐         │
       │          │Classical│         │
       │          │  Music  │         │
       │          └─────────┘         │
       ↓         ↙         ↘          ↓
    ┌──────────────────┐      ┌──────────┐
    │ Feminine Power   │ ←─── │  Indian  │
    │  and Rebellion   │      │  Music   │
    └──────────────────┘      └──────────┘
```

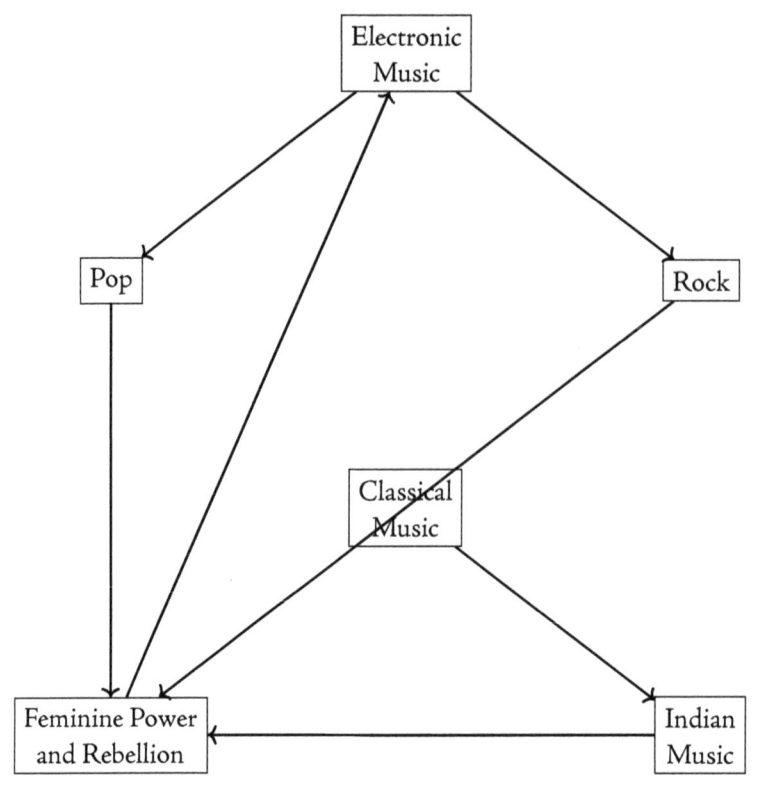

Krewella's musical influences are as diverse as their own backgrounds, weaving together classical, electronic, pop, rock, and Indian music into a unique and compelling mix. Their desire to break boundaries and embrace their feminine power sets them apart in the male-dominated EDM scene, inspiring both fans and fellow artists alike. By incorporating personal experiences and cultural heritage into their music, Krewella creates a powerful connection that resonates with audiences worldwide.

Finding Their Sound

The journey of any music band starts with a search for their unique sound, their own distinctive style that sets them apart from the rest. For Krewella, this search was a fascinating exploration of different genres, sounds, and influences that would ultimately shape their identity as artists.

In their quest to find their sound, Jahan and Yasmine, the talented sisters behind Krewella, embarked on a musical adventure that took them through a vast variety of genres. From pop to rock, from hip-hop to electronic dance music (EDM), they delved into the realms of different styles, experimenting and learning along the way.

One principle that guided Krewella's search for their sound was the idea of pushing boundaries and breaking stereotypes. They wanted to create a music that defied categorization and challenged the norms of the industry. They were determined to color outside the lines and create a sonic experience that was uniquely their own.

The sisters drew inspiration from a multitude of sources. Their childhood influences played a significant role in shaping their musical taste. Growing up, they were exposed to a diverse range of music, thanks to their parents' eclectic collection. Everything from Indian classical music to classic rock became a part of their listening repertoire, and this rich blend of sounds would later find its way into their own compositions.

Moreover, Krewella looked up to artists who were unafraid to experiment and push the boundaries of their respective genres. They admired trailblazers like Madonna and David Bowie, who constantly reinvented themselves and challenged the status quo. This spirit of artistic exploration became a driving force behind their search for a unique sound.

The duo also found inspiration in the rich tapestry of electronic dance music. The vibrant EDM scene in their hometown of Chicago provided them with a fertile ground for experimentation. They immersed themselves in the pulsating beats, infectious melodies, and electrifying energy of the EDM community, drawing inspiration from both local talents and international superstars.

One of the challenges they faced was finding a way to merge their love for diverse genres and create a cohesive sound that represented their identity. It required striking a delicate balance between their diverse influences and their vision for the future of their sound. They experimented with different production techniques, exploring various harmonic structures and rhythmic patterns to find the perfect fusion of their musical interests.

As they honed their skills and developed their sound, Krewella began to cultivate their own signature style, characterized by a seamless blend of pop sensibilities, rock influences, and the high-energy electronic elements of EDM. Their music became known for its anthemic choruses, powerful vocals, and infectious melodies that had the power to captivate audiences and create an immersive experience.

To further refine their sound, Krewella embraced collaboration. They recognized the power of working with other talented artists, as each collaboration brought new perspectives and expanded their sonic palette. By combining their abilities and ideas with those of others in the industry, they were able to explore new musical territories and continuously evolve their sound.

In their search for their sound, Krewella discovered that the essence of their music lied in channeling their authentic selves. They realized that their unique experiences, emotions, and stories were the key ingredients that would make their sound truly resonate with their audience. By infusing their music with their personal narratives, they were able to create a deep connection with their fans, who found solace and inspiration in the honesty of their lyrics and the rawness of their performances.

Ultimately, Krewella's journey of finding their sound was not just about the music but also about self-discovery. It was a process of soul-searching, experimenting, and embracing their individuality as artists. Through their relentless pursuit of their sound, they were able to carve out a distinct and dynamic place in the ever-evolving landscape of the music industry.

The Formation of Krewella

Let's dive into the electrifying story of how Krewella came to be. It all started with two fierce and talented sisters, Jahan and Yasmine, who were destined to create music that would disrupt the scene like a bolt of neon lightning.

A Musical Dream Awakens

As young girls growing up in a bustling Chicago suburb, Jahan and Yasmine were surrounded by a symphony of sounds. From the smooth rhythm of jazz to the soulful melodies of R&B, music had always been woven into the fabric of their lives. It was their personal escape, a sanctuary where they could let their imaginations run wild.

The sisters discovered their shared passion for music at a young age, often spending countless hours jamming together in their makeshift bedroom studio. Jahan, with her bewitching vocals, and Yasmine, with her innate talent for tinkering with electronic beats, found solace and inspiration in this creative collaboration.

Dreaming and Defying Conventions

As they grew older, Jahan and Yasmine refused to confine themselves to the stereotypes and conventions that society had set for them. Their rebellious spirits pushed them to think outside the box and create something unique, something that would shake the foundation of the music industry.

They experimented with different genres, blending elements of electronic, pop, and alternative rock to create a sound that was distinctly their own. They crafted intricate melodies and heart-pounding beats that brought goosebumps to even the most devout music listeners.

Neon Vibes and Collaborative Magic

To bring their vision to life, the Krewella sisters sought out like-minded souls who shared their vision and passion for music. The search led them to connect with Rain Man, a gifted producer who added a touch of magic to their already vibrant sound.

The synergy between Jahan, Yasmine, and Rain Man was undeniable. With their powers combined, they harmonized in perfect unison and created a sonic explosion that captivated the hearts and souls of audiences across the globe.

Rise of the Krew

With their unique sound firmly in place, Krewella burst onto the music scene like a supernova. Their energetic live performances, infused with raw emotion and pure adrenaline, left audiences craving more. They unleashed a wave of energy that reverberated through the hearts of their fans, creating an unbreakable bond between them.

Their infectious tracks, such as "Alive" and "Enjoy the Ride," exploded like fireworks, igniting dance floors worldwide. The Krewella phenomenon took hold, and fans couldn't get enough of their fearless and rebellious spirit.

Conquering Hearts and Shattering Expectations

As they navigated the ever-evolving sea of music, Krewella shattered expectations and proved that they were a force to be reckoned with. They fearlessly confronted the male-dominated industry, empowering women everywhere to break free from societal norms and embrace their true passions.

Their music became a sanctuary, a means for fans to escape the challenges of their own lives and feel the exhilaration of being alive. Krewella became more than just a band; they became a movement, a source of inspiration that transcended borders and united people from all walks of life.

But their journey was far from over. Challenges lay ahead, and in the next chapter, we'll explore how Krewella rose to stardom, defying the odds and leaving an indelible mark on the world of electronic dance music.

Chapter Two: Rise to Stardom

In Chapter Two, we delve into the extraordinary rise of Krewella as they explode onto the global stage, leaving an electrifying impact on the EDM scene. Discover how they harnessed the power of social media, conquered the Billboard charts, and embarked on exhilarating tours alongside EDM superstars. We'll explore the accolades and controversies that shaped their journey, highlighting their unique sound and unrivaled stage presence. Join us as we unravel the breathtaking story of Krewella's ascent to stardom.

The Early Days of Krewella

Ah, the early days of Krewella, where the stars were just starting to align and the music was just starting to burst into life. It was a time of passion, determination, and a whole lot of sisterly love. Let's dive into the world that birthed the iconic Krewella and explore the vibrant energy that set them on their extraordinary journey.

The Krewella Sisters: Jahan and Yasmine

Our story begins with two remarkable sisters, Jahan and Yasmine, who would soon become the creative powerhouse that is Krewella. These two badass ladies definitely didn't start their musical journey in the conventional way. Born into a Pakistani-American family, they grew up in the suburbs of Chicago, constantly challenging societal expectations and forging their own path.

Jahan, the older of the two, always had a flair for the dramatic. From a young age, she excelled in theater and dance, displaying a natural talent for performance. Yasmine, the younger sister, was a rebellious spirit with an insatiable appetite for music. Little did they know that their distinct personalities and shared love for music would converge to create something truly extraordinary.

A Musical Childhood

Music was in their blood, ingrained in their very existence. Growing up, the sisters were exposed to a diverse range of musical styles, thanks to their father's extensive record collection. From classic rock legends like Led Zeppelin and Pink Floyd to the soulful beats of Pakistani Qawwali music, their childhood was a melting pot of sonic inspiration.

Jahan and Yasmine embraced this diversity, allowing it to shape their musical tastes and fuel their creative fire. They became consumed by the power of music, spending countless hours exploring new sounds, dissecting lyrics, and analyzing the intricate melodies that resonated deep within their souls.

Influences and Inspirations

Every great artist is influenced by those who came before them, and Krewella is no exception. As they delved deeper into the world of electronic music, the sisters found themselves drawn to the infectious energy of acts like Pendulum, Modestep, and Skrillex. These artists pushed boundaries, blending genres and redefining the limits of what electronic music could be.

But it wasn't just the music that captivated Jahan and Yasmine. They were also inspired by the fearless attitude and unapologetic self-expression of iconic female musicians like Madonna and Gwen Stefani. These fierce women shattered stereotypes, paving the way for the Krewella sisters to break free from societal expectations and forge their own path in the male-dominated world of EDM.

Finding Their Sound

With a world of influences at their fingertips, Jahan and Yasmine set out to find their sound, determined to create something that was uniquely Krewella. They experimented with different genres, blending elements of electronic dance music, rock, and pop to craft their signature sound.

Drawing from their individual strengths, Jahan's powerful vocals and Yasmine's innate talent for production, they began to create music that spoke to a new generation. Their tracks were fueled by raw emotion, infused with the spirit of rebellion and empowerment. With every beat, they were building the foundation of a movement that would soon shake the music industry to its core.

The Formation of Krewella

The formation of Krewella was a moment of undeniable destiny. It was during a family vacation in 2007 that the sisters decided to embark on this musical journey together. And with that, Krewella was born.

Their bond as sisters provided the framework for their collaboration. They shared a deep understanding of one another, a telepathic connection that allowed their creative visions to merge seamlessly into a unified force. But it wasn't just about the music; it was about something bigger. Krewella became a symbol of sisterhood and empowerment, a platform to push boundaries and inspire others to embrace their true selves.

The Early Days of Krewella

In the early days, Krewella faced the same struggles that any emerging artist encounters. They hustled tirelessly, playing small gigs in Chicago's underground scene while juggling day jobs to make ends meet. The recognition they craved seemed elusive, but they refused to let setbacks deter them.

Their breakthrough came when they released their debut self-released EP, *Play Hard*, in 2011. It was a game-changer, capturing the attention of music lovers worldwide. With tracks like "Killin' It" and "Alive," Krewella unleashed a wave of infectious energy that resonated with fans on a visceral level.

Capturing the Chicago Scene

As their music began to gain traction, Krewella found themselves at the heart of Chicago's thriving music scene. The city's vibrant EDM community embraced them with open arms, recognizing their talent and fearless approach to music-making.

They quickly built a loyal following, who eagerly packed out every show, hungry for the raw electricity that defined a Krewella performance. Through their explosive live shows, Krewella brought the energy of the underground scene to the forefront, filling venues with a pulsating kaleidoscope of lights, beats, and pure unadulterated passion.

From Underground to Mainstream

Krewella was a force to be reckoned with, and it wasn't long before the music industry took notice. Major labels came knocking at their door, seeking to harness the untamed energy of Krewella and bring it to the masses.

But the sisters were determined to maintain creative control. They decided to form their own independent label, Mixed Kids Records, allowing them to preserve their unique sound and fiercely protect their artistic integrity. This bold move solidified their status as trailblazers, unafraid to challenge the status quo and pave their own way.

The Rise of EDM

Krewella's emergence coincided with the rise of electronic dance music, a genre that was gaining momentum on a global scale. They found themselves at the forefront of this movement, leading the charge with their electrifying live performances and genre-defying sound.

EDM was more than just a genre; it was a culture, a community of music lovers united by a shared love for the freedom of expression that electronic music provided. Krewella became the voice of a generation, embracing this newfound platform to spread their message of empowerment, love, and unbridled self-acceptance.

And so, the early days of Krewella were filled with passion, determination, and a burning desire to forge their own path. They had not yet reached the pinnacle of their success, but the seeds of greatness had been sown. Little did they know that their music would go on to touch the lives of millions, leaving an indelible mark on the music industry and inspiring a new generation of artists to dare to be different.

Capturing the Chicago Scene

The vibrant city of Chicago has always been a melting pot of diverse cultures and artistic expression. It's a city that thrives on creativity and pushes boundaries in various art forms, including music. For Krewella, capturing the essence of the Chicago scene was a pivotal moment in their journey.

Growing up in the suburbs of Chicago, Jahan and Yasmine were exposed to a rich musical heritage. From blues and jazz to house and hip-hop, the sounds of the city resonated with them from an early age. They were captivated by the energy and raw emotion that infused the local music scene.

A Musical Melting Pot

Chicago's music scene is a true melting pot, bringing together a diverse range of genres and artists. From the iconic blues clubs on the South Side, like Buddy Guy's Legends, to the underground hip-hop scene in the city's neighborhoods, Chicago offers a stage for musicians of all styles to showcase their talents.

Krewella immersed themselves in the local music scene, attending concerts, festivals, and underground shows. They absorbed the energy and passion of the musicians they encountered, soaking in the sounds and rhythms that defined the Chicago scene. From the pulsating beats of house music in clubs like The Mid, to the gritty punk rock shows at legendary venues like Metro, Krewella's musical journey was influenced by it all.

The DIY Spirit

The Chicago music scene is known for its DIY (do-it-yourself) ethos. It's a city where artists take matters into their own hands and create opportunities for themselves. Krewella embraced this spirit wholeheartedly, recognizing that success in the music industry would require more than just talent.

They started by performing at small local venues, building a loyal following one show at a time. The sisters took charge of their own promotion, creating a strong online presence through social media platforms like MySpace and YouTube. They leveraged the power of the internet to connect with fans and spread their music far beyond the confines of the Chicago scene.

Collaborations and Connections

One of the defining aspects of the Chicago music scene is the sense of community. Musicians collaborate, support each other, and inspire one another to push their boundaries. Krewella recognized the importance of building connections with like-minded artists and producers.

Through their involvement in the Chicago scene, Jahan and Yasmine met and collaborated with local talent, including DJ duo Flosstradamus and dubstep producer Kill the Noise. These collaborations not only expanded their musical horizons but also forged lasting friendships.

The Grit and Resilience

The Chicago music scene is not for the faint of heart. It's a scene that requires grit, determination, and a willingness to embrace the challenges that come with pursuing a career in music. Krewella learned this firsthand as they faced the ups and downs of trying to make it in a competitive industry.

They encountered countless rejections and setbacks, but they persevered. They drew inspiration from the proud history of Chicago musicians who had faced similar struggles and emerged victorious. The city's resilience and tenacity became embedded in Krewella's DNA, fueling their drive to succeed.

Pushing Boundaries and Creating New Sounds

As Krewella navigated the Chicago scene, they realized that to truly capture its essence, they needed to push boundaries and create a sound that was uniquely their own. They blended elements of their diverse musical influences, adding a electronic dance music (EDM) twist to create a fresh, innovative sound.

By experimenting with different genres and infusing their music with personal stories and emotions, Krewella captured the spirit of the Chicago scene while simultaneously pushing it forward. Their ability to seamlessly blend genres and create music that resonated with a wide audience set them apart from their peers.

Lessons from the Chicago Scene

The Chicago music scene taught Krewella invaluable lessons that would shape their trajectory as artists. It taught them the importance of community, collaboration, and resilience. It showed them that success requires embracing the DIY mentality and never giving up on their dreams.

The experiences and influences they absorbed from the Chicago scene laid the foundation for their future endeavors. They carried these lessons with them as they ventured beyond the city limits and forged their path on the global stage.

In capturing the essence of the Chicago scene, Krewella not only honored their musical roots but also paved the way for a new generation of artists to find their unique voice and make their mark on the world stage.

Overall, the section "1.1.7 Capturing the Chicago Scene" explores the impact of the vibrant and diverse music scene in Chicago on Krewella. It delves into the musical melting pot that exists in the city, the DIY spirit embraced by artists, the power of collaborations and connections, the grit and resilience required to make it in the Chicago scene, and the importance of pushing boundaries and creating a unique sound. This section underscores the valuable lessons that Krewella learned from their experiences within the Chicago scene and how it shaped their journey as musicians.

From Underground to Mainstream

Ah, the journey from underground to mainstream, an exhilarating rollercoaster ride that every band dreams of. And Krewella's story is no exception. Strap yourself in and hold on tight as we delve into the wild ride that brought this dynamic duo from the depths of the underground music scene to the glitzy stages of the mainstream.

The Early Days of Krewella

Like most success stories, Krewella's path to stardom was not paved with gold from the beginning. In fact, Jahan and Yasmine, the talented sisters behind Krewella, had to work tirelessly to establish themselves as a force to be reckoned with in the music industry.

Picture this: dimly lit underground clubs, pulsating beats, and a small but passionate crowd. This is where Krewella first cut their teeth, honing their skills and experimenting with different sounds. These early days were a crucial period of artistic exploration and self-discovery for the sisters.

Capturing the Chicago Scene

Chicago, the birthplace of house music, played a pivotal role in shaping Krewella's unique sound. The sisters embraced the city's vibrant underground scene, soaking up its energy and incorporating it into their music.

They frequented legendary venues like The Mid and Spybar, where they carved out their space in the local scene. Their energetic performances and boundary-pushing tracks quickly caught the attention of the Chicago music community.

The Rise of EDM

As Krewella honed their craft, a larger phenomenon was taking place: the rise of Electronic Dance Music (EDM). The electronic music scene was rapidly gaining popularity, fueled by festivals, such as Ultra Music Festival and Electric Daisy Carnival, and the infectious beats of producers like Skrillex and Deadmau5.

Krewella found themselves in the midst of this EDM explosion, and their unique blend of genres, combining elements of electronic, pop, and rock, set them apart from the crowd.

Underground Success

With their growing popularity in the underground scene and their undeniable talent, Krewella started attracting attention from record labels. But they were determined to do things their way, maintaining their independence and creative control.

They opted to release their music themselves, leveraging the power of social media and the internet to connect directly with their fans. Through platforms like SoundCloud and YouTube, Krewella cultivated a loyal following, spreading their music like wildfire and gaining recognition beyond the confines of the underground.

Mainstream Breakthrough

But it was their breakout single, "Alive," that propelled Krewella into the mainstream spotlight. The infectious anthem, with its anthemic chorus and infectious melodies, caught the ears of music lovers worldwide.

"Alive" quickly climbed the charts, peaking at number 32 on the Billboard Hot 100. Suddenly, Krewella was no longer just an underground sensation; they had crossed over into the mainstream, capturing the hearts of listeners everywhere.

Chart-Topping Success

With their newfound mainstream success, Krewella continued to dominate the charts. Their debut album, "Get Wet," debuted at number eight on the Billboard 200, solidifying their place as a musical force to be reckoned with.

Songs like "Live for the Night" and "Enjoy the Ride" became anthems for a generation, blurring the lines between genres and captivating audiences with their infectious energy.

Embracing the Mainstream

While some bands may struggle with the transition from underground to mainstream, Krewella embraced the opportunity with open arms. They recognized that their unique sound had the power to resonate with a broader audience, and they were determined to make their mark on the music world.

They continued to push boundaries, infusing their tracks with a raw, in-your-face energy that captivated listeners. And as they embraced the mainstream, they never lost sight of their roots, always staying true to their underground origins.

Critics and Controversies

Of course, with success comes criticism, and Krewella was no stranger to controversy. As their popularity grew, so did the scrutiny and the pressure to conform to certain expectations.

They faced backlash from purists who accused them of selling out and abandoning their underground roots. But Krewella remained unapologetically themselves, refusing to be confined by others' expectations.

The Krewella Sound

What sets Krewella apart and contributed to their success is their ability to seamlessly blend genres, creating a sound that is uniquely their own. Their music is a fusion of catchy pop hooks, hard-hitting electronic beats, and emotionally-charged lyrics.

Whether you're in a crowded club or driving with the windows down, Krewella's music has a way of capturing your attention and making you lose yourself in the moment. It's an addictive blend that has garnered them a dedicated fan base and continues to draw listeners from all walks of life.

So, there you have it—the thrilling journey that took Krewella from the underground to the mainstream. It's a story of talent, perseverance, and a refusal to conform. But their journey doesn't stop here. Krewella continues to evolve and push boundaries, leaving their mark on the music industry, one electrifying track at a time. And who knows where their incredible journey will take them next?

Now, hold on tight as we dive into the next chapter of Krewella's odyssey: Rise to Stardom. Stay tuned, music lovers!

The Rise of EDM

The rise of Electronic Dance Music (EDM) in recent years has been nothing short of extraordinary. This genre, characterized by its infectious beats, pulsating rhythms, and electrifying energy, has taken the music industry by storm and captured the hearts of millions around the world. In this chapter, we peel back the layers of this phenomenon and explore the factors that contributed to its meteoric rise.

The Birth of a Movement

EDM traces its roots back to the underground music scene of the 1980s, where pioneers like Kraftwerk, Giorgio Moroder, and Juan Atkins laid the groundwork for what would become a global phenomenon. Drawing inspiration from various genres such as disco, synth-pop, and techno, these trailblazers paved the way for the emergence of a new sound that would come to define an entire generation.

Technological Advancements

One of the key catalysts for the rise of EDM was the rapid advancement of technology. The advent of affordable and accessible music production software, coupled with the rise of the internet and digital streaming platforms, democratized music creation and distribution. This allowed aspiring artists to experiment with sounds, collaborate across borders, and reach a global audience like never before.

The Power of Social Media

In an era dominated by social media, platforms like SoundCloud, YouTube, and Twitter became virtual stages for aspiring EDM artists to showcase their talent. With a few clicks, bedroom producers could upload their tracks, gain exposure, and amass a dedicated following. This direct connection between artists and fans fuelled the growth of EDM, creating a community-driven movement that celebrated creativity and innovation.

The Festival Experience

EDM festivals emerged as epicenters of the genre's explosion, providing a communal space for fans to immerse themselves in the music and culture. Events like Ultra Music Festival, Electric Daisy Carnival, and Tomorrowland not only showcased the biggest names in EDM but also served as platforms for up-and-coming artists to make their mark. The electrifying atmosphere, jaw-dropping production, and the collective experience of thousands of fans dancing in unison cemented EDM's position as a cultural force to be reckoned with.

Blurring of Genre Boundaries

EDM's rise to prominence can also be attributed to its ability to transcend genre boundaries. Artists began incorporating elements from various genres - hip-hop, rock, pop, and even classical music - into their productions, pushing the boundaries of what EDM could be. This fusion of different styles and influences not only attracted a diverse audience but also kept the genre fresh and relevant.

The Global Dance Movement

EDM's meteoric rise was not limited to any particular region. Instead, it spread like wildfire across the globe, captivating audiences from Europe to Asia, from the Americas to Africa. The universal appeal of EDM, coupled with the infectious energy of its live performances, led to a wave of sold-out shows, massive fanbases, and a growing acceptance of the genre within mainstream music circles.

Challenges and Criticisms

As EDM gained mainstream popularity, it also faced its fair share of challenges and criticisms. Detractors argued that the genre was formulaic, lacking in depth and artistic value. Others criticized the commercialization of EDM, pointing to the rise of superstar DJs and the emphasis on spectacle over substance. However, proponents of the genre countered that EDM was more than just the "drop," highlighting the emotional connection, escapism, and sense of community that it provided.

The Future of EDM

Looking ahead, the future of EDM seems bright. As technology continues to evolve, artists are constantly exploring new ways to push the boundaries of sound and live performances. The genre's global influence shows no signs of waning, as new festivals, events, and artists continue to emerge around the world.

In this chapter, we have laid the foundation for understanding the rise of EDM. From its humble beginnings in underground clubs to its current status as a global cultural phenomenon, this genre has proven its resilience and staying power. In the next chapter, we delve deeper into the journey of Krewella and their role in shaping the landscape of EDM.

Chapter Two: Rise to Stardom

Signing with Krewella

The Breakthrough Moment

The journey of Krewella has been filled with ups and downs, but no moment in their career has been more impactful than their breakthrough moment. It was the turning point that catapulted them from hopefuls in the EDM scene to rising stars that captured the attention of fans worldwide. This section takes a closer look at the defining moment that changed everything for Jahan and Yasmine - the Krewella sisters.

A Dream Becoming Reality

Like many aspiring musicians, Jahan and Yasmine had a dream. They dreamed of making music that would resonate with people, that would touch their souls and make them feel alive. The sisters had been honing their skills and developing their sound for years, but it was always a struggle to get their music out into the world. They knew they had something special, but they needed the right opportunity to showcase it.

The Call That Changed Everything

One fateful day, Jahan and Yasmine received a call that would change their lives forever. It was a call from a renowned music producer who had stumbled upon their music online. He was captivated by their unique sound, their infectious energy, and their undeniable talent. He saw something in them that he knew the world would love.

Signing with Krewella

The music producer wasted no time in offering Jahan and Yasmine a record deal. It was an opportunity of a lifetime, a chance to turn their dreams into reality. They were ecstatic and couldn't believe that their hard work had finally paid off. With excitement and nerves, they signed the contract and officially became Krewella.

The Power of Social Media

But signing with a record label was just the beginning. The real breakthrough moment came when Krewella discovered the power of social media. They realized that they had a unique opportunity to connect directly with their fans, to share their music and their journey in a way that had never been done before. They embraced platforms like Twitter, Facebook, and YouTube to build a loyal and passionate fan base.

Earning Recognition in the EDM Community

Krewella's breakthrough moment came when they released their first official single. The EDM community, hungry for fresh and innovative music, embraced Krewella with open arms. Their single quickly gained traction and became a hit on radio stations and music charts worldwide. DJs around the globe started playing their tracks in their sets, and Krewella's name began to spread like wildfire.

The Impact of "Play Hard"

The breakthrough moment reached its climax with the release of Krewella's breakout track, "Play Hard." This electrifying anthem captured the energy and spirit of a generation. It became an instant hit, resonating with fans and critics alike. "Play Hard" catapulted Krewella into the spotlight, solidifying their status as rising stars in the EDM world.

Touring with EDM Superstars

As word of Krewella's talent and electrifying live performances spread, they had the opportunity to tour with some of the biggest names in the EDM scene. Sharing the stage with renowned artists like Skrillex and David Guetta, Krewella proved that they belonged among the elite. Their breakthrough moment was not just about the success of a single, but also about showcasing their talent to a global audience.

The Release of "Get Wet"

After their breakthrough moment, Krewella was riding an unstoppable wave of success. They seized the opportunity and released their debut album, "Get Wet." This album was a collective representation of their journey, their struggles, and their resilience. It showcased their evolution as artists and solidified their place in the music industry.

The Billboard Hot 100

Krewella's breakthrough moment was further validated when their music started climbing the charts. They achieved the remarkable feat of reaching the prestigious Billboard Hot 100, a milestone that represented their growing popularity and the impact of their music on a mainstream level. This achievement was a testament to their talent and the sheer force of their breakthrough moment.

Criticisms and Controversies

With success comes scrutiny, and Krewella faced their fair share of criticisms and controversies. Some accused them of selling out or abandoning their underground roots. But the sisters remained steadfast in their pursuit of their unique sound and their vision for Krewella. They weathered the storm and emerged stronger than ever.

Krewella's Unique Sound

What set Krewella apart from other EDM acts was their ability to blend different genres and create a sound that was distinctly their own. Their breakthrough moment not only marked their rise to stardom but also showcased their unique sound. With their powerful vocals, infectious melodies, and hard-hitting beats, Krewella created a fusion of electronic, pop, and rock that resonated with a wide audience.

In conclusion, the breakthrough moment for Krewella was a culmination of years of hard work, dedication, and unwavering belief in their music. It was the moment when they went from being just two sisters with a dream to being international stars in their own right. Their unique sound, combined with the power of social media and the support of their fans, propelled them to new heights and solidified their place in the music industry. The breakthrough moment was just the beginning of their incredible journey, foreshadowing the success, challenges, and ultimately, the enduring legacy of Neon Frequencies.

The Power of Social Media

In today's digital age, social media has become an integral part of our lives, shaping the way we communicate, connect, and consume content. For music artists like Krewella, social media has proven to be a powerful tool for building a dedicated fan base, expanding their reach, and shaping their brand.

Harnessing the Reach of Social Media

Jahan and Yasmine, the talented sisters behind Krewella, recognized early on the immense power of social media platforms in connecting with their fans. With platforms like Facebook, Twitter, and Instagram, they were able to showcase their unique blend of electronic dance music (EDM) and connect with fans on a global scale.

The sisters used these platforms to share their music, tour updates, and behind-the-scenes glimpses into their lives as musicians. By engaging with their fans directly through social media, they created a loyal community, fostering a sense of belonging and intimacy that extended beyond the music itself.

Building a Personal Connection with Fans

Social media provided Krewella with an unprecedented opportunity to interact with their fans on a personal level. Through thoughtful posts, live streams, and direct messaging, the sisters made an effort to respond to as many fans as possible, making each individual feel seen and valued.

By sharing their thoughts, experiences, and even personal challenges, Jahan and Yasmine were able to create a genuine connection with their fans. This level of accessibility allowed them to build strong relationships and establish a loyal fan base that felt invested not only in their music but also in their journey as artists and individuals.

Amplifying Music Releases and Live Performances

The power of social media extends beyond mere communication and interaction. Krewella understood that social media could be used as a platform to amplify their music releases and live performances, reaching a wider audience in an instant.

Prior to releasing their debut album "Get Wet," Krewella strategically used social media to generate hype and anticipation. They released teaser snippets, behind-the-scenes footage, and exclusive content, all designed to engage their fans and generate buzz. By doing so, they created a virtual community of fans eagerly awaiting the album's release.

During their live performances, Krewella would often leverage social media to maximize their reach. They encouraged fans to capture their experiences at concerts using designated hashtags, prompting others to join the conversation and creating a flood of user-generated content. This not only expanded Krewella's online presence but also added an element of inclusivity, ensuring that fans felt like an active part of the Krewella experience.

The Evolution of Social Media Marketing

With social media constantly evolving, Krewella has adapted their marketing strategies to stay relevant and engaged with their fan base. They have embraced new platforms such as TikTok, where they create short, entertaining videos to connect with a younger demographic.

Krewella also leverages the power of social media influencers, collaborating with popular content creators to promote their music and events. By tapping into the influencers' established fan base, Krewella is able to reach new audiences and extend their reach beyond traditional marketing channels.

Challenges and Ethical Considerations

While social media has undoubtedly been a game-changer for Krewella, it is not without its challenges and ethical considerations. The constant pressure to maintain an active online presence can be overwhelming, and the line between personal and public life can become blurred.

Krewella has navigated these challenges by prioritizing mental health and setting boundaries. They advocate for authenticity on social media, encouraging their fans to embrace their true selves instead of conforming to societal expectations. By being transparent about their own struggles, they aim to create a safe space where fans can feel accepted and supported.

Moreover, Krewella recognizes the importance of using their platform responsibly. They actively promote inclusivity, diversity, and equality, using their social media presence to advocate for social justice issues and connect with like-minded individuals and organizations.

Conclusion

The power of social media in the music industry cannot be overstated. For Krewella, it has been instrumental in building a dedicated fan base, amplifying their music releases, and creating a personal connection with their fans.

Whether it's engaging with fans directly, leveraging influencers, or adapting to new platforms, Krewella has harnessed the power of social media to establish themselves as a prominent force in the EDM scene. As they continue to evolve and navigate the ever-changing digital landscape, one thing is certain – social media will always be an integral part of their journey.

Earning Recognition in the EDM Community

When it comes to making a mark in the world of music, there's no denying that recognition is the name of the game. And for Krewella, earning recognition in the EDM community was a pivotal milestone in their journey. In this section, we'll explore how Jahan and Yasmine's unique style and unwavering dedication earned them the respect and admiration of their peers.

Finding their Sound

Before we delve into Krewella's rise to fame, it's important to understand how they crafted their distinct sound. Drawing inspiration from their diverse musical backgrounds, the Krewella sisters created a fusion of electronic music genres, infusing elements of dubstep, progressive house, and pop. Their ability to seamlessly blend these styles set them apart in the EDM scene.

Pushing Boundaries

One of the reasons why Krewella garnered recognition in the EDM community was their fearless approach to pushing boundaries. They were never ones to play it safe or follow trends. Instead, they were known for their experimental nature and willingness to explore new sonic territories.

For instance, Krewella's track "Killin' It" challenged the conventional EDM formula with its catchy pop hooks and powerful vocals. It showcased their ability to incorporate elements from different genres, earning them praise for their innovative sound.

Epic Live Performances

Another factor that contributed to Krewella's recognition in the EDM community was their legendary live performances. Jahan and Yasmine's high-energy stage presence, combined with their infectious music, captivated audiences around the world.

Their electrifying shows became the stuff of legends, with fans eagerly awaiting their next tour. Krewella's ability to create an immersive experience through their music and performance style solidified their place as rising stars in the EDM scene.

Collaborations with EDM Superstars

In the world of music, collaborations can often be a catalyst for gaining recognition. Krewella understood this, and they strategically teamed up with established EDM superstars to elevate their profile.

Working with the likes of Nicky Romero and Gareth Emery allowed Krewella to tap into a wider audience and gain the respect of their peers. These collaborations not only showcased their versatility as artists but also positioned them as serious contenders in the EDM community.

Consistent Output and Label Support

Earning recognition in any industry requires consistency and perseverance. Krewella understood this and consistently released new music to stay relevant and maintain their connection with fans. Their dedication to their craft was evident through the quality of their productions and the authenticity of their lyrics.

Moreover, Krewella's association with major record labels like Columbia Records and Ultra Records provided them with the necessary platform and resources to reach a wider audience. Label support played a vital role in amplifying their visibility in the EDM community, opening doors for collaborations and high-profile gigs.

Building a Strong Fan Base

Last but certainly not least, Krewella's recognition in the EDM community can be attributed to their loyal and dedicated fan base. From the early days, Jahan and Yasmine fostered a deep connection with their fans through social media and live interactions.

By actively engaging with their followers and showcasing appreciation for their support, Krewella created a community where fans felt valued and connected. This strong support system not only propelled their rise but also served as a testament to their authenticity and talent.

Unconventional but Relevant

In a world filled with conformity, Krewella's unconventional but relevant approach to music certainly played a role in earning them recognition. They didn't shy away from experimenting with different genres and styles, and their willingness to take risks paid off.

For example, Krewella's decision to release their music for free early on in their career was a bold move that demonstrated their focus on connecting with fans rather than chasing commercial success. This unconventional strategy helped them build a dedicated following and set them apart from their peers.

Summary

Earning recognition in the EDM community is no easy feat, but Krewella managed to do so with their unique style, boundary-pushing experimentation, epic live performances, strategic collaborations, consistent output, and strong connection with their fan base. Through their music, they made a lasting impact on the EDM scene and paved the way for future artists to take risks and find their own unique voice.

As we continue to explore Krewella's journey, we'll uncover the challenges they faced and the resilience they displayed in overcoming them. But for now, let's celebrate their recognition in the EDM community and the mark they made with their Neon Frequencies.

The Impact of "Play Hard"

Ah, "Play Hard." What a game-changer for Krewella and the EDM community as a whole! This electrifying anthem took the world by storm, leaving a lasting impact on music lovers everywhere. Let's dive into the seismic effect that "Play Hard" had on Krewella's career and the EDM landscape.

A Breath of Fresh Air

"Play Hard" burst onto the scene like a bolt of lightning, injecting a vibrant energy into the EDM genre. With its infectious beat, catchy lyrics, and electrifying drops, this track quickly became an anthem for party-goers and festival enthusiasts.

The song's pulsating energy transcended crowds and transcended borders, cementing Krewella's reputation as a force to be reckoned with. From the underground clubs of Chicago to the stages of international festivals, "Play Hard" became an instant hit, bringing Krewella into the spotlight and propelling them towards stardom.

Revolutionizing the EDM Sound

"Play Hard" wasn't just another hit song; it was a groundbreaking revolution in electronic dance music. Krewella's unique fusion of melodic dubstep, progressive house, and electro-pop elements created a sonic masterpiece that captured the hearts of millions.

This track showcased Krewella's ability to push boundaries and redefine the EDM sound. They seamlessly blended heavy basslines with soaring vocals, creating an unparalleled sonic experience that set them apart from their peers. "Play Hard" became a catalyst for experimentation within the genre, inspiring a new wave of artists to explore uncharted musical territories.

An Anthem of Empowerment

Beyond its infectious beat and innovative sound, "Play Hard" carried a powerful message of empowerment. Its lyrics spoke of breaking free from societal constraints, embracing individuality, and living life to the fullest.

This anthem resonated deeply with listeners, particularly with the younger generation who found solace in its message. It became a rallying cry for self-expression, a reminder to embrace one's true identity without fear of judgment.

Krewella's authenticity and fearlessness in embracing their own uniqueness inspired countless individuals to do the same. Through "Play Hard," they became torchbearers of empowerment, using their music as a vehicle for social change and acceptance.

A Global Phenomenon

"Play Hard" catapulted Krewella into the international spotlight, propelling them onto stages around the world and solidifying their status as global EDM superstars. The track's infectious melodies and high-energy drops captivated audiences at major festivals, including Ultra Music Festival, Electric Daisy Carnival, and Tomorrowland.

The song's impact extended far beyond the dancefloor. It dominated airwaves, climbed the charts, and earned Krewella a devoted international fan base. Thanks to "Play Hard," Krewella's music reached every corner of the globe, transcending cultural boundaries and resonating with fans from all walks of life.

Challenges and Criticisms

However, with great success came great scrutiny. As "Play Hard" garnered popularity, Krewella faced their fair share of criticisms and controversies. Some purists in the EDM community accused them of "selling out" and compromising the genre's authenticity.

Yet, Krewella remained resilient and unapologetic, staying true to their artistic vision and refusing to be confined by labels. They embraced the criticism as fuel for creativity, using it to drive their evolution and challenge the status quo.

The Enduring Legacy

As we reflect on the impact of "Play Hard," it's clear that this anthemic track left an indelible mark on both Krewella's career and the EDM landscape. It revolutionized the genre's sound, empowered a generation, and propelled Krewella towards international stardom.

But the legacy of "Play Hard" extends beyond its chart success and critical acclaim. Its enduring impact lies in the inspiration it continues to provide for artists, the empowerment it offers to fans, and the boundary-breaking spirit it represents within the ever-evolving EDM scene.

So, turn up the volume, let the beats pulse through your veins, and remember the impact that "Play Hard" had on the world of music. It's a testament to the power of Krewella's artistry and the unifying force of electronic dance music.

Now, let's move forward and explore the challenges and resilience that defined Krewella's journey in the next chapter of Neon Frequencies. Get ready to witness the transformative power of music and the unwavering spirit of two sisters who conquered the world, one electrifying track at a time.

Touring with EDM Superstars

The journey to success is often filled with incredible experiences and unforgettable moments. For the members of Krewella, touring with EDM superstars was one such experience that truly shaped their rise to stardom. In this section, we dive into the thrilling world of touring and the impact it had on Krewella's career.

The Power of Collaboration

Collaborations with established EDM superstars opened doors for Krewella and helped them gain recognition in the music industry. Joining forces with renowned artists such as Skrillex, Zedd, and Calvin Harris allowed Krewella to tap into their fan base and expand their reach to a wider audience.

Touring alongside these EDM giants not only gave Krewella exposure but also served as a learning experience. They were able to witness firsthand the professionalism, showmanship, and dedication required to perform at such high levels. These collaborations provided Krewella with the opportunity to study and refine their craft, pushing them to elevate their performances and musicality.

The Energy of Live Performances

One of the unique aspects of EDM music is its ability to electrify audiences through live performances. Krewella embraced this energy, delivering electrifying shows that resonated with fans worldwide. Their dynamic stage presence, infectious energy, and connection with the audience became the hallmark of their performances.

As Krewella toured with EDM superstars, they not only observed the energy of live performances but also honed their own stage presence. They learned to captivate audiences with their music, engaging them through interactive experiences and immersive visuals. Krewella's dedication to delivering exhilarating performances solidified their reputation as an unstoppable force in the EDM scene.

The Thrill of Festival Circuit

EDM festivals became a significant platform for Krewella to showcase their talent and connect with fans on a larger scale. With performances at renowned festivals such as Ultra Music Festival, Electric Daisy Carnival, and Tomorrowland, Krewella cemented their status as festival favorites.

The festival circuit allowed Krewella to share the stage with not only EDM superstars but also a diverse range of artists. This exposure to different genres and styles influenced their own sound, pushing them to experiment and innovate. Immersed in the pulsating energy of the festival crowds, Krewella continually pushed boundaries, blending genres and creating a unique sonic experience.

Balancing Fame and Performance

While touring with EDM superstars brought Krewella immense fame and success, it also came with its own set of challenges. The pressure to deliver powerful performances consistently turned into a balancing act between maintaining their artistic integrity and meeting audience expectations.

Krewella's journey taught them the importance of striking a balance between staying true to themselves and adapting to the demands of the industry. They navigated through criticisms, controversies, and high expectations with resilience, always striving to give their fans an unforgettable experience.

Touring Adventures and Misadventures

Life on the road is not without its share of adventures and misadventures. From lost baggage and missed flights to awe-inspiring encounters with fans, Krewella's touring experiences were a rollercoaster ride filled with memorable moments.

In the midst of hectic tour schedules, Krewella embraced the chaos and treated every setback as an opportunity for growth. These experiences not only shaped their perspective on the music industry but also strengthened their bond as sisters and artists.

Unconventional Wisdom: Embrace the Journey

Touring with EDM superstars taught Krewella one valuable lesson—music is not just about the destination but also the journey. They learned that success is not solely measured by record sales or chart positions but by the experiences, connections, and personal growth along the way.

Krewella's touring adventures became a testament to their unwavering passion and resilience. They embraced the ups and downs of the tour life, finding inspiration in every city, every performance, and every interaction. Through their journey, they discovered that the true essence of being an artist lies in the ability to create unforgettable moments and touch the lives of their fans.

Conclusion

Touring with EDM superstars was an integral part of Krewella's rise to stardom. It exposed them to new audiences, elevated their performances, and influenced their creative evolution. From collaborating with EDM icons to conquering the festival circuit, Krewella's touring experiences shaped their musical journey and contributed to their enduring legacy.

In the next chapter, we delve into the challenges and resilience that Krewella faced during their journey, exploring the personal struggles, turbulent relationships, and their unbreakable bond that propelled them forward. Stay tuned for the gripping revelations of their resilience and redemption in the face of adversity.

The Release of "Get Wet"

Let's dive into the exhilarating journey of Krewella and explore the release of their debut album, "Get Wet." This album marked a significant milestone in the career of the Krewella sisters, Jahan and Yasmine, propelling them into stardom and solidifying their presence in the electronic dance music (EDM) scene.

Setting the Stage

Before the release of "Get Wet," Krewella had already made a splash in the music industry with their infectious blend of electronic beats, powerful vocals, and catchy hooks. Tracks like "Alive" and "Killin' It" had already amassed a massive following, paving the way for their debut album to take the world by storm.

The Creative Process

Creating an album is never an easy task, and "Get Wet" was no exception. Jahan and Yasmine poured their hearts and souls into crafting a musical experience that would captivate their fans and resonate with listeners worldwide.

The creative process of "Get Wet" was a true expression of Krewella's dynamic and versatile style. From the high-energy anthems to the emotionally charged ballads, the album showcased their ability to experiment with different sounds and genres while staying true to their unique identity.

Unleashing the Beast

On September 24, 2013, "Get Wet" hit the shelves and digital platforms, igniting a frenzy among fans who had been eagerly anticipating its release. The album delivered an electrifying collection of tracks that seamlessly blended elements of dubstep, house, and pop.

The lead single, "Live for the Night," became an instant hit, serving as a powerful anthem and an invitation for fans to embrace the wild and carefree nature of Krewella's music. Its infectious chorus and pulsating beats had partygoers across the globe dancing to the rhythm of their rebellious hearts.

Collaborations and Musical Chemistry

"Get Wet" also showcased Krewella's penchant for collaborations, teaming up with talented artists to infuse their music with fresh perspectives and diverse influences. The album featured collaborations with Pegboard Nerds, Gareth Emery, and Patrick Stump of Fall Out Boy, among others.

These collaborations not only added depth and variety to the album but also highlighted the chemistry and camaraderie between Krewella and their fellow musicians. Each track was a testament to their ability to merge different artistic visions seamlessly and create something truly magical.

Connecting with the Fans

One of the defining aspects of Krewella's journey has been their deep connection with their fans. "Get Wet" solidified this bond through its relatable lyrics, powerful melodies, and empowering messages. Tracks like "This Is Not the End" and "We Go Down" resonated with listeners on a personal level, serving as anthems for anyone navigating through the ups and downs of life.

Krewella didn't just release an album; they created a community. Their music became more than just a soundtrack; it became a source of inspiration, a support system, and a platform for self-expression.

Critics and Success

With any album release comes the scrutiny of critics, and "Get Wet" faced its fair share of both acclaim and criticism. Some praised the album for its infectious energy, genre-bending sound, and the sisters' undeniable talent, while others criticized it for straying too far from traditional EDM conventions.

Regardless of the critical reception, "Get Wet" enjoyed immense success. It peaked at number eight on the Billboard 200 chart and reached the top spot on the Billboard Dance/Electronic Albums chart. The album's success solidified Krewella's status as a force to be reckoned with in the EDM industry.

An Unforgettable Era

"Get Wet" not only marked a milestone for Krewella but also for the EDM genre as a whole. The album's success opened doors for other EDM artists, pushing the boundaries of what was considered mainstream and blazing a trail for future generations.

Through the release of "Get Wet," Krewella immersed their audience in a euphoric experience. They created a sonic landscape where listeners could escape the ordinary and embrace the extraordinary. The album's impact was felt not only in the music industry but also in the hearts and minds of their fans.

An Unconventional Approach

In true Krewella fashion, their journey to the release of "Get Wet" was filled with unconventional yet rewarding decisions. From their unique sound to their relentless pursuit of creative freedom, Jahan and Yasmine refused to conform to the industry's expectations, opting instead to carve their own path.

Their unapologetic attitude resonated with fans worldwide, inspiring them to embrace their individuality and challenge societal norms. Krewella's journey serves as a reminder that staying true to oneself and embracing the unconventional can lead to groundbreaking success.

Evolving Soundscapes

"Get Wet" marked the beginning of a new era for Krewella, setting the stage for their evolving soundscapes in the years to come. The album served as a launchpad for the duo's exploration of new sounds, genres, and collaborations, showcasing their versatility as artists and their commitment to growth.

As we close this chapter on the release of "Get Wet," we can't help but be captivated by the relentless passion, fearless innovation, and unwavering dedication that define Krewella's journey. Their story is a testament to the power of music and the transformative impact it can have on both artists and their fans.

In the next section, we will delve into the challenges and resilience that Krewella faced on their path to success, exploring the personal struggles, bond of sisterhood, and creative evolution that shaped their remarkable journey. Stay tuned for the next chapter of Neon Frequencies!

The Billboard Hot 100

The Billboard Hot 100 is the ultimate musical battleground, where artists from all genres fight for chart domination and bragging rights. It's the holy grail of music rankings, the one that separates the chart-toppers from the rest of the pack. And in 2013, Krewella made their mark on this prestigious chart with their infectious hit single, "Alive."

The Birth of "Alive"

"Alive" was the brainchild of Krewella, a high-energy, electronic dance music trio consisting of sisters Jahan and Yasmine, along with their partner, Rain Man. The track was released as the lead single from their debut studio album, "Get Wet," and it took the music world by storm.

The Rise on the Charts

When "Alive" hit the Billboard Hot 100, it quickly started climbing the ranks. Within weeks of its release, the song broke into the top 40, joining the likes of pop icons such as Katy Perry and Bruno Mars. But Krewella didn't stop there. With relentless energy and countless hours spent promoting their music, they kept pushing "Alive" higher and higher.

A Breakthrough Moment

After weeks of dedication and hard work, Krewella achieved a major milestone. "Alive" cracked the top 10 of the Billboard Hot 100, cementing its place as one of the most successful EDM tracks of the year. The infectious melodies, electrifying beats, and empowering lyrics resonated with fans across the globe.

The Power of Radio

While Krewella's dedicated fan base played a huge role in propelling "Alive" up the charts, the song's success was also fueled by heavy radio airplay. Stations from coast to coast, both mainstream and alternative, recognized the track's undeniable appeal and added it to their playlists. This exposure allowed Krewella's music to reach a wider audience, spanning beyond the boundaries of the EDM scene.

The Impact

Krewella's incredible rise on the Billboard Hot 100 was a testament to their unique sound and undeniable talent. They not only brought EDM to the mainstream but also challenged the traditional boundaries of genre classification. Their ability to seamlessly blend elements of EDM, rock, and pop attracted a diverse fan base and made them stand out in a crowded music landscape.

Unconventional Promotion

One of the secrets to Krewella's success was their unconventional approach to promotion. They leveraged the power of social media to connect directly with their fans, building a strong and loyal community. From behind-the-scenes studio footage to impromptu live performances, Krewella made sure their audience felt like they were a part of the journey.

Keeping it Real

While the Billboard Hot 100 success was undoubtedly a significant achievement for Krewella, they remained true to their roots throughout the entire process. They never lost sight of their love for the music and their desire to create an authentic connection with their fans. This genuine passion is what continues to set them apart in the industry.

The Formula to Success

Krewella's success on the Billboard Hot 100 didn't happen overnight. It was the result of relentless determination, a unique sound, and strategic moves. Here are some key factors that contributed to their rise:

Infectious Hooks

"Alive" had an undeniable hook that hooked the listeners right from the start. The chorus was catchy, anthemic, and instantly memorable. Krewella understood the power of a killer hook and made sure to deliver one that would stay in their fans' heads long after the song ended.

Emotional Resonance

Beyond its infectious beats, "Alive" also struck a chord with listeners on an emotional level. The powerful lyrics conveyed a message of resilience and empowerment, making it a relatable anthem for anyone going through tough times. Krewella's ability to combine emotional depth with electrifying energy resonated deeply with their audience.

Versatility

Krewella's ability to infuse different elements into their music was key to their success. Their tracks appealed to both EDM enthusiasts and casual listeners, bridging the gap between genres. By incorporating elements of rock and pop into their electronic sound, they created a unique and versatile style that had mass appeal.

Live Performances

Krewella's electrifying live performances also played a crucial role in their rise. Their energy on stage was unmatched, and they made sure every audience member felt like they were part of an unforgettable experience. The duo's infectious enthusiasm and stage presence left fans craving more and helped solidify their status as a must-see act.

The Unconventional Path

Krewella's journey to the top of the Billboard Hot 100 was far from conventional. They faced their fair share of challenges and setbacks along the way, but they never let those obstacles define them. Their relentless pursuit of their dreams, combined with their willingness to embrace unconventional strategies, paved the way for their remarkable success.

Pushing Boundaries

Krewella understood that to make it big, they needed to push boundaries and challenge the status quo. They weren't afraid to blur genre lines, experiment with different sounds, and collaborate with artists from diverse backgrounds. This fearlessness allowed them to carve out a unique niche for themselves in the music industry.

Connecting with Fans

Krewella's connection with their fans went beyond just making music. They made a conscious effort to engage with their audience through various platforms, including social media, live streams, and meet-and-greets. By building authentic relationships with their fans, they created a loyal and dedicated community that stood by them through thick and thin.

Staying True to Themselves

Throughout their journey, Krewella remained fiercely true to themselves. They never compromised their artistic vision or tried to fit into a predetermined mold. Their authenticity and unapologetic approach to their music were the driving forces behind their success. By staying true to who they were, they inspired countless others to embrace their own uniqueness.

Lessons Learned

Krewella's success on the Billboard Hot 100 is not just a testament to their talent, but also a source of inspiration for aspiring musicians. Here are some key lessons we can take away from their story:

Embrace Your Uniqueness

Don't be afraid to be different. Your unique sound and perspective are what will set you apart from the crowd. Embrace your individuality and use it to your advantage.

Connect with Your Audience

Your fans are your biggest advocates. Take the time to build genuine connections with them and make them feel like they're part of something special. Engage with them on social media, interact at shows, and show them that their support matters.

Stay True to Yourself

Never compromise your artistic vision or change who you are to fit into someone else's idea of success. Stay true to yourself and your beliefs, and the right audience will find you.

Be Bold and Fearless

Don't be afraid to take risks and step outside of your comfort zone. The path to success is rarely a straight line, so embrace the unknown and be willing to push boundaries.

Work Hard and Stay Focused

Success doesn't come easy. It takes dedication, hard work, and a relentless drive. Stay focused on your goals and never lose sight of the passion that fuels your music.

Conclusion

Krewella's remarkable journey on the Billboard Hot 100 is a testament to the power of determination, authenticity, and a unique sound. From their breakthrough hit "Alive" to their relentless pursuit of success, they have inspired countless musicians and fans alike. As they continue to evolve and push the boundaries of electronic dance music, there's no doubt that Krewella will leave an enduring legacy in the music industry. So, keep your ears open and get ready to experience the unstoppable force that is Krewella.

Criticisms and Controversies

Ah, criticism and controversy, the spicy ingredients that make up the cocktail of fame. Krewella, being not your average band, has had its fair share of both. Let's dive into the tumultuous world of Krewella and explore some of the criticisms and controversies that have surrounded their journey.

One of the major criticisms thrown at Krewella was their transition from underground to mainstream. Some fans accused them of "selling out" and compromising their unique sound to appeal to a wider audience. Critics argued that their early hits, such as "Killin' It" and "Alive," were raw and genuine, while their later tracks lacked the same edge and authenticity. The band responded to these claims by asserting their artistic growth and experimentation, defending their decision to explore different genres and styles.

But it wasn't just their music that faced scrutiny. Krewella's image and public persona also drew criticism. Some critics accused the band of relying heavily on their sex appeal, suggesting that their success was due to their looks rather than their talent. Detractors argued that their stage outfits and provocative music videos overshadowed their artistry, undermining their credibility as serious musicians. This criticism struck a chord with the band, prompting them to address the issue head-on. They explained that their image was a reflection of their unapologetic, confident personalities and that they were proud to embrace their femininity and sexuality.

Controversy, like the cherry on top, often accompanies criticism, and Krewella has certainly had its fair share. One of the most prominent controversies was the departure of Kris "Rain Man" Trindl from the band in 2014. The split was highly publicized, leading to finger-pointing and a messy legal battle. Trindl claimed that he had been forced out by the sisters, while Jahan and Yasmine defended their decision, stating that it was due to Trindl's struggle with addiction and his inability to contribute to the band's creative process. This controversy not only tested the sister's bond but also made headlines, shining a spotlight on the challenges that come with being in the music industry.

Another controversy that ignited strong reactions was Krewella's outspoken political views and activism. The sisters used their platform to support causes such as LGBTQ+ rights, women's empowerment, and immigration reform, which garnered both praise and backlash. Some fans admired their courage and saw them as leaders in a male-dominated industry, while others accused them of being out of touch with their fans and forcing their beliefs on others. Krewella stood their ground, encouraging open dialogue and staying true to their values, even in the face of criticism.

Amidst the turmoil, Krewella's unique sound faced its fair share of controversy as well. Critics argued that their music lacked substance and depth, cherry-picking catchy melodies over meaningful lyrics. However, the band defended their approach, citing the power of music to uplift and unite, regardless of its perceived simplicity. They emphasized that their primary goal was to create an emotional connection with their audience and provide an energetic and unforgettable live experience.

As with any art form, criticisms and controversies come with the territory. Krewella has weathered the storm with resilience and determination, using each challenge as an opportunity for growth and self-reflection. Their ability to tackle controversies head-on while staying true to their vision has only strengthened their bond as a band and solidified their place in the ever-evolving music scene.

Well, that concludes our exploration of the criticisms and controversies surrounding Krewella's journey. Stay tuned for the next chapter, where we dive into the challenges and resilience that shaped their path to success!

Krewella's Unique Sound

When it comes to the music of Krewella, one thing is for certain – their sound is undeniably unique. Blending elements of electronic dance music, pop, and rock, Krewella has managed to create a style that is entirely their own. In this section, we will delve into the various aspects that contribute to Krewella's distinctive sound and explore the innovative techniques they employ in their music.

EDM with a Twist

At its core, Krewella's sound is rooted in electronic dance music (EDM). However, what sets them apart from other EDM artists is their ability to infuse different genres seamlessly. They blend hard-hitting beats, catchy hooks, and infectious melodies with elements of rock and pop, creating a sound that is both edgy and accessible.

One of the key elements that contribute to Krewella's unique sound is their exceptional songwriting. Jahan and Yasmine, the Krewella sisters, are not only talented vocalists but also gifted songwriters. They draw inspiration from personal experiences, emotions, and social issues, crafting lyrics that resonate with their audience on a deep level.

Diverse Musical Influences

Krewella's diverse musical influences play a significant role in shaping their sound. Growing up, Jahan and Yasmine were exposed to a wide range of music genres, from rock and metal to hip-hop and pop. These influences are apparent in their music, as they effortlessly incorporate elements from different genres into their songs.

Additionally, Krewella draws inspiration from various cultures and musical traditions. Having Indian-Pakistani heritage, they infuse elements of South Asian music into their tracks, incorporating traditional instruments, melodies, and vocal techniques. This blend of cultural influences adds further depth and richness to their sound.

Experimental Production Techniques

Krewella's sound is also characterized by their innovative and experimental production techniques. They constantly push the boundaries of electronic music, utilizing unconventional sounds and effects to create a unique sonic experience.

One notable aspect of Krewella's production is their use of aggressive and distorted synths. These powerful and gritty sounds add intensity and energy to their music, setting them apart from other EDM artists who may opt for cleaner, more polished sounds.

Krewella also employs complex layering techniques, combining different vocal harmonies, melodies, and textures to create a full and immersive sound. This meticulous attention to detail ensures that each of their tracks is a sonic journey that captivates the listener from start to finish.

The Krewella Experience

Beyond their music, Krewella's unique sound is also a result of the energetic and unforgettable live performances they deliver. Known for their high-octane shows filled with stunning visuals and immersive stage design, Krewella takes their audience on a sonic and visual journey like no other.

Their live performances incorporate elements of rock concerts, with Jahan and Yasmine showcasing their incredible vocal prowess while also playing live instruments such as drums and guitar. This combination of live instrumentation with electronic elements enhances their sound and adds a raw and organic dimension to their music.

Krewella's Impact on EDM

Krewella's unique sound has made a significant impact on the EDM scene. They have inspired a new generation of artists to explore and experiment with different genres, pushing the boundaries of electronic music even further.

Their ability to seamlessly blend different musical styles and cultures has also challenged stereotypes within the industry. As female artists in a predominantly male-dominated field, Krewella has proven that gender is not a limitation when it comes to creating groundbreaking music.

With their empowering lyrics, infectious melodies, and innovative production, Krewella has created a sound that defies categorization and resonates with listeners around the world. Their unique blend of EDM, pop, rock, and cultural influences has allowed them to carve out a distinctive place in the music industry, leaving a lasting impact on the genre and setting the stage for the future of electronic dance music.

Chapter Three: Challenges and Resilience

The Price of Fame

The Pressure to Perform

Being in the music industry is no easy feat. From the moment they burst onto the scene, Krewella has felt the weight of the world on their shoulders. They were not just another band, but pioneers of electronic dance music (EDM). With their unique sound, energetic performances, and vibrant personalities, they quickly gained a massive following and became a force to be reckoned with.

But with fame comes pressure, and Krewella soon found themselves facing the overwhelming expectations of their growing fan base and the music industry. The pressure to perform at a certain level, maintain their creative edge, and constantly deliver hit songs became a constant challenge for the young sisters.

One of the main sources of pressure for Krewella was the demand for their live performances. EDM is a genre known for its high-energy shows, explosive visual effects, and crowd interaction. Fans flocked to Krewella's shows not just to hear their music, but to experience an unforgettable spectacle. This created a delicate balance for the band - they had to constantly push the boundaries of their performances while staying true to their own artistic vision.

To meet these demands, Jahan and Yasmine had to dedicate countless hours to rehearsals and stage preparation. They worked tirelessly to perfect their performances, ensuring that every movement, every beat drop, and every visual element was flawlessly executed. This required immense physical and mental stamina, as well as a deep understanding of the technical aspects of their shows.

But the pressure to perform was not just limited to their live shows. It extended to every aspect of their career, from songwriting to recording to promotion. Krewella's fans expected them to consistently release new and innovative music that would keep them at the top of the charts. This meant that Jahan and Yasmine had to constantly challenge themselves creatively, pushing their boundaries and exploring new musical territories.

In addition to the external pressures, Krewella also put immense pressure on themselves. They were perfectionists who always aimed for the highest standards in their work. This internal drive pushed them to constantly strive for improvement and to never settle for mediocrity. They wanted their fans to experience their music in the most authentic and powerful way possible.

However, the pressure to perform didn't come without its challenges. It took a toll on the sisters both physically and mentally. The constant touring, late nights, and demanding schedules left them exhausted and in desperate need of rest. Balancing their personal lives and relationships with their professional commitments became a delicate juggling act.

To cope with the pressure, Krewella turned to various means of self-care and relaxation. They prioritized their mental and physical well-being, making sure to take breaks when needed and surround themselves with a support system of friends and family. They also found solace in their art, using music as a form of therapy and expression.

Despite the challenges, Krewella managed to rise above the pressure and continue to deliver extraordinary performances. They found strength in their passion for music and in the unwavering support of their fans. They learned to embrace the challenges and use them as fuel for their creative fire.

The pressure to perform will always be a part of Krewella's journey. It is something they have learned to navigate and harness to their advantage. Their resilience and determination have allowed them to not just survive, but thrive in the music industry. And through it all, they have remained true to themselves and their music, inspiring a new generation of artists and leaving a lasting legacy in the world of EDM.

Personal Struggles and Addiction

Life in the spotlight can often take a toll on even the strongest individuals, and the sisters of Krewella were not exempt from the challenges that fame brings. As they soared to new heights in their music careers, Jahan and Yasmine faced personal struggles and battled addiction along the way.

The Dark Side of Success

With fame comes pressure, and the pressure to constantly perform and meet high expectations can be overwhelming. Jahan and Yasmine found themselves grappling with the dark side of success as they tried to navigate the demanding music industry.

The Pressure to Perform

Every song, every album, and every live performance carried with it the weight of impressing their fans and proving their worth. The pressure to constantly deliver new and innovative music, while also maintaining their high-energy live shows, began to take a toll on the sisters.

In the quest to keep up with the demands, they found themselves trapped in a cycle of stress and anxiety. The need to continually produce hit songs and perform flawlessly left little room for rest and self-care.

Personal Struggles and Addiction

Underneath the glitz and glamour of the music industry, Jahan and Yasmine were battling their own personal demons. Like many musicians, they turned to substances as a way to cope with the challenges they faced.

The music industry can be a breeding ground for addiction, with temptations lurking at every turn. Substance abuse became a crutch for Jahan and Yasmine as they sought solace in a world that often felt chaotic and overwhelming.

Breaking the Cycle

Recognizing the destructive path they were on, Jahan and Yasmine made the courageous decision to seek help and break free from their addictions. They understood that their personal struggles not only jeopardized their own well-being but also the future of Krewella.

Rehabilitation became a turning point in their lives, and they emerged with newfound clarity and determination. They acknowledged the strength of their bond as sisters and as a musical duo and vowed to support each other through the highs and lows.

The Road to Recovery

Recovery is a journey, and Jahan and Yasmine embarked on this path with a renewed sense of purpose. They surrounded themselves with a strong support system of friends, family, and professionals who helped guide them toward healing.

With addiction in their rearview mirror, Jahan and Yasmine embraced a healthier lifestyle, paying attention to their physical and mental well-being. They refused to let their past struggles define them, but instead used their experiences to fuel their creativity and passion for music.

Spreading Awareness

Having overcome their personal battles, Jahan and Yasmine became advocates for addiction recovery and mental health. They shared their stories openly, breaking down the stigma surrounding addiction and inspiring others to seek help.

Through their music and public speaking engagements, the sisters encouraged their fans to prioritize self-care and mental well-being. They stressed the importance of asking for help when needed and reminded their audience that reaching out is a sign of strength, not weakness.

The Unbreakable Bond of Sisterhood

Jahan and Yasmine's journey through personal struggles and addiction ultimately strengthened their bond as sisters. They learned the importance of supporting each other unconditionally and faced their challenges side by side.

The power of sisterhood became evident not only in their personal lives but also in their music. Their shared experiences gave birth to lyrics that resonated with millions of fans, creating a deep connection between Krewella and their audience.

The Light at the End of the Tunnel

Personal struggles and addiction tested the resilience of the sisters, but it also served as a catalyst for growth and transformation. Through their pain, Jahan and Yasmine found the strength to rise above their circumstances and create a brighter future for themselves and their music.

The journey to recovery was not easy, but it ultimately led them to a place of redemption and reconnection. Their shared experiences shaped them not only as individuals but also as artists, and their music became a beacon of hope and inspiration for those facing similar battles.

The story of personal struggles and addiction within Krewella serves as a reminder that no one is immune to the challenges of life. It is a testament to the power of resilience, the strength of sisterhood, and the ability to turn adversity into triumph.

Turbulent Relationships Within the Group

Ah, relationships within a group - the stuff of legends. We've all heard the stories of bands who couldn't stand each other but somehow managed to create magic on stage. Well, Krewella is no exception to this rule. Behind the scenes, the sisters Jahan and Yasmine have weathered their fair share of storms, testing the strength of their bond and the very foundation of the group.

You see, being in a band is like being in a marriage, without the sexy parts. It requires constant communication, compromise, and understanding. Throw in the pressure of the music industry, long hours on the road, and the general craziness of the EDM world, and you have a recipe for fireworks. And not the good kind.

When it comes to turbulent relationships within the group, Krewella has experienced their fair share of ups and downs. There were times when tensions ran high, creative differences flared, and they wondered if the band would ever make it out alive. But through it all, they managed to find a way back to each other, stronger and more determined than ever.

One of the major challenges they faced was the clash of creative visions. Jahan and Yasmine have always been fiercely independent and strong-willed. They each brought their own musical influences and ideas to the table, sometimes leading to heated debates and conflicts. It's like arguing over whether pizza or tacos is the superior food (everyone knows it's pizza, by the way). But seriously, when you're so passionate about your craft, it's natural to clash with others who are equally as passionate.

To navigate these rough waters, Krewella had to find a way to compromise. They learned to listen to each other's ideas with an open mind, respecting each other's artistic perspectives. It wasn't always easy, but they discovered that the magic happens when you find the middle ground, combining the best of both worlds into something extraordinary. It's like adding pineapple to your pizza - controversial, but surprisingly delicious.

Another challenge that tested the sisters' relationship was the constant pressure to perform at their best. The demand for Krewella's music was sky high, and they had to constantly push themselves to meet those expectations. The stress of living up to their fans' and industry's standards took a toll on their personal lives and tested their emotional resilience.

There were moments when the pressure became too much, leading to personal struggles and addictive behaviors. They found solace and escape in substances that only magnified their problems. It was a dark period for the group, a time when they felt like they were losing control of everything they had worked so hard to build.

But here's the thing about Krewella - they're fighters. They refused to let their personal demons tear them apart. With the support of their loved ones and a kick-ass support team, they overcame their addictions and faced their inner demons head-on. It wasn't easy, and the road to recovery is never a straight line, but they emerged stronger and more determined to stay united as a band.

Through their journey, Krewella discovered that turbulent relationships within a group are not weaknesses, but opportunities for growth. It forced them to confront their own flaws, communicate openly, and truly understand each other's pain and struggles. The bond between Jahan and Yasmine became unbreakable, a foundation that could weather any storm.

And let's not forget the power of love. Love for the music they create, the fans who support them, and most importantly, the love they have for each other as sisters. Love has a funny way of healing wounds and bringing people back together. It's like a musical superpower that can overcome any obstacle.

So, what's the lesson here? Turbulence within a band is inevitable, but it's how you navigate those rough patches that truly defines the strength of the group. It's about finding common ground, respecting each other's individuality, and most importantly, never losing sight of the love and passion that brought you together in the first place.

Krewella's story of turbulent relationships within the group is a testament to the power of resilience, communication, and the unbreakable bond between sisters. It's a reminder that even in the chaos, beautiful music can be created, and dreams can be realized.

So, when you find yourself at odds with your bandmates, remember Krewella's journey. Embrace the turbulence, work through the challenges, and always come back to the love that brought you together. Who knows, you might just create something extraordinary in the process.

And with that, we leave you with a quote from Jahan and Yasmine themselves: "In the end, it's all about the music and the love we share. That's what keeps us going, even when the seas get rough."

Krewella's Unbreakable Bond

At the heart of Krewella's success lies the unbreakable bond between Jahan and Yasmine Yousaf, the talented sisters who make up the core of the band. Their connection as siblings and best friends has been the driving force behind their journey in the music industry. In this section, we will delve into the unique dynamics of their relationship, which has played a significant role in shaping Krewella's identity and resilience.

THE PRICE OF FAME

The Yousaf sisters share a deep and profound understanding of each other, which stems from their childhood experiences and the shared pursuit of their musical dreams. Growing up in a tight-knit Pakistani-American family, Jahan and Yasmine were exposed to a myriad of musical influences from a young age. Their father, who was an accomplished musician, exposed them to diverse genres, ranging from classical Pakistani music to classic rock and electronic dance music. This early exposure set the stage for their future as artists and sparked their passion for creating music that defies genre boundaries.

From their earliest memories, Jahan and Yasmine have found solace and inspiration in music, using it as a means of self-expression and a way to navigate life's ups and downs. Their shared experiences of growing up in a multi-cultural household and the challenges they faced as first-generation Americans created a deep understanding and empathy between the sisters. This shared background has been a driving force behind their determination to make a mark in the music industry and serve as role models for others of diverse backgrounds.

As they forged their path in the music industry, the Yousaf sisters faced numerous obstacles and setbacks. From the intense competition and critics in the industry to personal struggles and addiction, their bond proved to be their greatest source of strength. They relied on each other for guidance, support, and motivation, even during the toughest times. Together, they weathered the storms and emerged even stronger, using their shared experiences to fuel their art and create music that resonates with their fans.

The unbreakable bond between Jahan and Yasmine became the backbone of Krewella's creative process. Their ability to communicate openly and honestly about their innermost thoughts and emotions allowed them to craft songs that are deeply personal and relatable. Through their music, they have shared their vulnerabilities, insecurities, and triumphs, creating a powerful connection with their audience.

Despite the challenges and pressures of being in the spotlight, Jahan and Yasmine have managed to maintain their strong bond, always putting their relationship and shared vision for Krewella at the forefront. Their commitment to each other and the band has been unwavering, even in the face of adversity. This unbreakable bond has allowed them to evolve as artists and navigate the ever-changing landscape of the music industry.

In the process of creating their music, Jahan and Yasmine have developed a symbiotic relationship where they complement each other's strengths and weaknesses. While Jahan brings a fierce and powerful vocal range to the table, Yasmine's skills as a producer and songwriter add depth and complexity to their sound. This synergy between their musical talents has been a driving force behind

Krewella's unique and captivating sound.

Their collaboration goes beyond just the creative aspect of their music. Jahan and Yasmine share a vision for Krewella that extends beyond their performances and extends to their impact on the world. They have used their platform to advocate for important causes, including gender equality, mental health awareness, and LGBTQ+ rights. Through their music and activism, they have become role models for aspiring artists and have inspired a new generation to pursue their dreams fearlessly.

The unbreakable bond between Jahan and Yasmine has been the foundation of Krewella's success and resilience. Their shared experiences, unwavering support for one another, and commitment to their art have allowed them to overcome challenges and carve out a unique place in the music industry. As Krewella continues to evolve and push boundaries, their unbreakable bond will undoubtedly remain at the core of their success.

Going the Extra Beat

Just like the unbreakable bond between Jahan and Yasmine, Krewella's music is all about breaking barriers and pushing boundaries. One way they achieve this is by incorporating unconventional elements into their sound. For instance, they fuse traditional Pakistani music with electronic beats, creating a style that is uniquely their own. This fusion not only adds depth and richness to their music but also serves as a celebration of their heritage and a way to connect with their global audience.

In addition to their unique sound, Krewella also experiments with unconventional song structures and production techniques. They are known for their energetic and high-octane performances, which often feature unexpected drops, intricate vocal arrangements, and intense build-ups. This level of innovation and creativity sets them apart from other artists in the EDM genre and keeps their audience on the edge of their seats.

Krewella's commitment to breaking barriers also extends to their live performances. They have incorporated live instrumentation into their sets, allowing them to create a dynamic and immersive experience for their fans. From live drums to guitar solos, these elements add an extra layer of excitement and authenticity to their shows, making them unforgettable experiences.

Through their commitment to pushing boundaries and experimenting with unconventional elements, Krewella continues to captivate audiences and redefine what it means to be an EDM artist. Their unbreakable bond and fearless approach to music-making ensure that they will continue to make waves in the industry for years to come.

A New Direction and Creative Evolution

Amidst the challenges and setbacks faced by Krewella, Jahan and Yasmine found themselves at a crossroads in their musical journey. They realized that in order to move forward and reignite their passion for music, they needed to take a new direction and embark on a path of creative evolution.

Exploring New Musical Genres and Collaborations

To embrace this new direction, Krewella started exploring different musical genres beyond their signature electronic dance music (EDM) sound. They wanted to push their boundaries and experiment with fresh, captivating sounds that would surprise their fans and inspire them to think outside the box.

One of the most notable aspects of Krewella's creative evolution was their collaboration with artists from diverse genres. They understood that by collaborating with musicians from different backgrounds, they could infuse their music with a unique blend of styles and create something truly extraordinary.

Imagine this: Jahan and Yasmine teaming up with a renowned hip-hop artist to create a track that seamlessly blends EDM and rap. The combination of pulsating beats, energetic drops, and clever rap verses would create a dynamic, genre-defying sound that would captivate both EDM enthusiasts and hip-hop fans alike.

Krewella's willingness to experiment and collaborate across genres opened up a world of possibilities for their music. They found themselves immersed in a creative melting pot where boundaries dissolved and innovation thrived.

Embracing Live Instruments and Orchestral Arrangements

In their quest for a new musical direction, Krewella also decided to incorporate live instruments and orchestral arrangements into their productions. They recognized that by bringing in the rich, organic sound of instruments, they could add depth and emotion that couldn't be replicated solely through electronic means.

Picture this: Jahan and Yasmine, surrounded by a full orchestra, playing their electrifying melodies alongside soaring strings, melodic woodwinds, and powerful brass sections. The fusion of electronic elements with the grandeur of a symphony orchestra would create a sonic experience that would transport their audience to another dimension.

This unconventional approach to their music presented both technical and creative challenges for Krewella. They had to carefully orchestrate and arrange their compositions, ensuring that the electronic elements seamlessly intertwined with the live instruments. This process required meticulous attention to detail, as they sought to create a harmonious balance between the raw energy of EDM and the sophistication of orchestral music.

Concept Albums and Visual Storytelling

Krewella's new direction extended beyond just the music itself; they wanted to create a complete sensory experience for their fans. They began exploring the concept of concept albums, where each album tells a cohesive story and takes listeners on a journey from start to finish.

Imagine this: Krewella releasing an album that not only showcases their evolving musical style but also presents a captivating narrative. Each track would be a chapter in a larger story, with the overall album weaving together a tale of personal growth, transformation, and resilience.

To complement their musical storytelling, Krewella also delved into the world of visual storytelling. They collaborated with talented visual artists and directors to create mesmerizing music videos and live visual performances. These visuals enhanced the narrative of their concept albums, bringing their music to life in a visually stunning and emotionally evocative way.

Pushing Boundaries: The Convergence of Music and Technology

True to their innovative spirit, Krewella embraced the convergence of music and technology as a means to push boundaries and further expand their creative evolution. They recognized the power of immersive experiences and sought to leverage technology to engage their fans in unprecedented ways.

Imagine this: Jahan and Yasmine incorporating virtual reality (VR) into their live performances, allowing fans to step into their world and experience their music from a completely immersive perspective. VR headsets would transport fans to a virtual concert venue, where they could interact with virtual avatars of Krewella, dancing alongside them as they perform their electrifying tracks.

Krewella also explored the use of augmented reality (AR) in their music releases, offering fans the opportunity to unlock hidden content and engage with interactive elements through their mobile devices. By scanning album covers or posters, fans could reveal behind-the-scenes footage, exclusive interviews, and even enter virtual worlds inspired by Krewella's music.

This convergence of music and technology not only allowed Krewella to connect with fans on a deeper level but also showcased their ability to adapt and embrace the ever-changing landscape of the music industry.

The Audacity to Innovate: Redefining their Sound

Through their new direction and creative evolution, Krewella showed the world that they were never content with complacency. They dared to challenge conventions and redefine their sound, continuously pushing the boundaries of what EDM could be.

Their music became a testament to their resilience, their ability to adapt, and their unwavering commitment to artistic growth. With each new release, Krewella invited their fans to join them on a journey of discovery, where they could explore uncharted territories and witness the metamorphosis of two fearless musicians.

In a world where artistic stagnation can lead to mediocrity, Krewella remained true to their bold spirit, embracing change and emerging stronger than ever before.

Exercises

1. Think about your favorite music genre. How could you combine it with another genre to create a unique, genre-defying sound? Describe the elements from each genre that you would incorporate into your composition.

2. Research a concept album from an artist you admire. Analyze how the individual tracks contribute to the overall narrative and the emotions they evoke. Create a playlist that follows a narrative structure and tells a coherent story.

3. Experiment with incorporating a live instrument into an electronic music production. Choose an instrument and try adding it to your composition. How does the instrument change the overall mood and feel of the track?

4. Reflect on the impact of technology on the music industry. How has it changed the way artists create and engage with their audience? Brainstorm innovative ways technology could be further integrated into the music experience.

5. Imagine you are a visual artist collaborating with a musician to create a music video. Brainstorm ideas for visually representing the emotions and narrative of a song. Consider the use of symbolism, color palettes, and visual effects to evoke specific feelings in the viewer.

Key Takeaways

- Embracing a new direction and creative evolution can reignite passion and push artistic boundaries. - Collaboration with artists from diverse genres can lead to unique and genre-defying compositions. - Incorporating live instruments and orchestral arrangements adds depth and emotion to electronic music. - Concept albums and visual storytelling create a complete sensory experience, engaging listeners on multiple levels. - Pushing the convergence of music and technology allows for innovative fan engagement and immersive experiences. - Daring to redefine one's sound demonstrates resilience and an unwavering commitment to artistic growth in a rapidly changing industry.

Collaborations and Experimentations

Collaborations have played a pivotal role in Krewella's musical journey, allowing them to explore different genres, experiment with new sounds, and push the boundaries of their creativity. In this section, we delve into some of their most notable collaborations and the impact they had on Krewella's music.

One of Krewella's early collaborations that gained significant attention was their partnership with electronic music producer and DJ, Nicky Romero. The resulting track, "Legacy," showcased the seamless blend of Krewella's powerful vocals and Romero's infectious melodies, creating a high-energy anthem that resonated with fans worldwide. The success of "Legacy" not only solidified Krewella's presence in the EDM scene but also highlighted their ability to collaborate with industry heavyweights while maintaining their unique sound.

Continuing their exploration of collaborations, Krewella joined forces with the Los Angeles-based producer, Adventure Club, for the track "Rise & Fall." This collaboration allowed Krewella to dive into the realms of melodic dubstep, combining emotional lyrics with heavy bass drops. The vulnerable yet empowering message of "Rise & Fall" resonated deeply with fans, cementing Krewella's reputation as artists who fearlessly address themes of resilience and personal growth.

Krewella's willingness to experiment with diverse musical styles and collaborate with artists outside the EDM genre is evident in their collaboration with Indonesian rapper, Rama Davis, on the track "Team." This unexpected collaboration effortlessly fused EDM with elements of hip-hop, showcasing the sisters' ability to adapt their sound while still staying true to their signature style. "Team" garnered widespread praise for its infectious energy and powerful message of unity and self-empowerment.

In addition to external collaborations, Krewella has also explored the concept of internal collaborations within their own music production. This includes working closely with other talented producers to create a cohesive sound. One notable example is their collaboration with longtime friend and producer, Pegboard Nerds. Together, they created the track "Another Round," which seamlessly combines Krewella's melodic sensibilities with Pegboard Nerds' distinctive, high-energy style. This collaboration not only showcased their ability to work well with others but also demonstrated their commitment to pushing boundaries and exploring new sonic territories.

In their pursuit of musical innovation, Krewella has also ventured into the realm of live instrumentation in their performances and studio recordings. This experimentation adds a dynamic and organic element to their electronic sound, diversifying their musical palette and capturing the essence of their high-energy live performances.

Despite facing criticism for their genre-blending approach, Krewella has remained steadfast in their commitment to collaborations and experimentations. They believe that music is an ever-evolving art form that should be constantly explored and reinvented. Their collaborations have allowed them to redefine genre boundaries, break free from constraints, and continue to push the envelope of what is possible in the EDM world.

In conclusion, collaborations and experimentations have been integral to Krewella's artistic growth and success. Their willingness to collaborate with diverse artists and explore new sounds has not only expanded their musical horizons but also allowed them to connect with a broader audience. By embracing these experiences, Krewella has solidified their position as innovators in the EDM scene and paved the way for future artists to challenge conventions and create music that defies categorization.

The Release of "Ammunition EP"

The release of "Ammunition EP" marked a significant milestone in the journey of Krewella, showcasing their growth, evolution, and relentless pursuit of artistic expression. In this chapter, we delve into the inspiration behind this explosive EP, its impact on the music industry, and the innovative approaches that Krewella employed.

Unleashing Creative Freedom

"Ammunition EP" represented a turning point for Krewella, as it marked their first independent release. Free from the constraints of a major record label, Jahan and Yasmine were able to fully embrace their creative instincts and deliver a project that truly represented their artistic vision.

The EP served as a testament to their refusal to conform to industry norms and their determination to carve their own distinctive path. It embodied the essence of Krewella's rebellious spirit, pushing sonic boundaries and expanding the horizons of electronic dance music.

An Experimental Sound

With "Ammunition EP", Krewella ventured into new sonic territories, exploring a diverse range of genres, encompassing elements of dubstep, trap, and pop. This experimentation allowed them to create a body of work that defied categorization and resonated with a wide audience.

The EP is a sonic kaleidoscope that takes listeners on an exhilarating journey through pulsating beats, infectious melodies, and thought-provoking lyrics. Tracks like "Beggars" blend aggressive basslines with emotive vocals, creating an anthemic experience that resonates with the listeners' deepest emotions.

A Personal Catharsis

"Ammunition EP" reflects the personal struggles and triumphs that Jahan and Yasmine experienced during a transformative period of their lives. Through their music, they channeled their innermost emotions, transforming pain into power and adversity into art.

The raw and introspective nature of the EP allowed fans to connect with Krewella on a deeply personal level. Tracks like "Can't Forget You" drew from the pain of lost love, while "Broken Record" conveyed the intensity of personal battles and the resilience that emerges from facing them head-on.

Revolutionizing the Release Strategy

In addition to its groundbreaking content, Krewella revolutionized the way music was released in the digital age with "Ammunition EP". They employed an innovative approach, choosing to release each track individually over a span of six months, building anticipation and keeping their audience engaged.

This unconventional strategy allowed fans to fully immerse themselves in each track, fostering a sense of excitement and connection with the music. Furthermore, it demonstrated Krewella's commitment to defying traditional industry norms and embracing the limitless possibilities offered by the digital landscape.

Empowering the Live Experience

With "Ammunition EP", Krewella aimed to create an EP that transcended the studio, energizing their live performances and captivating audiences around the world. They meticulously crafted each track, infusing them with an electrifying energy that resonated with fans during their energetic and visually stunning live shows.

The EP became the foundation for their awe-inspiring global tour, with tracks like "Marching On" and "Surrender the Throne" becoming anthems that unified crowds and ignited a collective sense of empowerment. Krewella's ability to create an immersive and electrifying live experience became their trademark, setting them apart from their peers in the EDM scene.

Legacy and Impact

The release of "Ammunition EP" cemented Krewella's place as pioneers of electronic dance music, presenting a new standard for artistic freedom, creative experimentation, and boundary-pushing innovation. It served as a bold statement of their unwavering commitment to authenticity and sonic exploration.

Moreover, the EP inspired a new generation of artists to defy the confines of mainstream culture and push the boundaries of their own creativity. It became a testament to the power of resilience and perseverance, demonstrating that true artistry is born from embracing one's unique voice and fearlessly venturing into uncharted territory.

As we turn the page on this chapter in Krewella's journey, we cannot help but marvel at the impact and enduring legacy of "Ammunition EP". Its release marked a pivotal moment for Krewella, shaping their career and the trajectory of electronic dance music itself. Through their music, Jahan and Yasmine continue to empower listeners, reminding us that we all have the ammunition within us to conquer any obstacle life throws our way.

On a Personal Note

As I delve into the captivating story of Krewella, I am reminded of the importance of pursuing our passions relentlessly and embracing our unique voice. The release of "Ammunition EP" serves as a reminder that true artistry stems from the courage to challenge the status quo and create work that speaks to the depths of our souls.

In the next chapter, we explore the challenges and triumphs that propelled Krewella towards their global success. We unravel the personal struggles, the unbreakable bond that kept them together, and the creative evolution that defined their journey. Join me as we dive deeper into the whirlwind world of Krewella and discover the incredible story of resilience and reinvention.

The Rebirth of Krewella

After facing numerous challenges and setbacks, Krewella found themselves at a crossroads. It seemed like their dream was slipping away, and they were on the verge of giving up. But true to their resilient spirit, Jahan and Yasmine refused to let adversity define them. Instead, they embraced the opportunity for rebirth, both as individuals and as a band.

Redefining Their Purpose

During this pivotal moment, Jahan and Yasmine took a step back to reflect on their journey and reassess their goals. They realized that they had lost sight of why they started making music in the first place. It wasn't about fame or fortune; it was about the love and connection they felt when creating and sharing their music with others.

They also recognized the need to reconnect with their fans on a deeper level. It was time to break down the barriers that had formed between Krewella and their supporters, and to rebuild a sense of trust and authenticity.

Rediscovering Their Sound

In their quest for rebirth, Krewella embarked on a musical exploration, diving into uncharted territories. They experimented with different genres, blending elements of pop, rock, and electronic music. This marked a turning point for the band, as they discovered a newfound freedom in their creative expression.

By pushing the boundaries of their sound, Krewella reinvented themselves, shedding their old sonic identity and embracing a more mature and sophisticated approach. They crafted deeply personal and introspective lyrics, allowing their audience to truly connect with their music on an emotional level.

Embracing Collaboration

Another key aspect of Krewella's rebirth was their openness to collaboration. They understood that by working with others, they could bring fresh perspectives and elevate their music to new heights. They sought out talented artists and producers who shared their vision, creating a space for collective creativity to thrive.

This collaborative spirit also extended to their live performances. Krewella invited guest artists to join them on stage, bringing diverse musical influences and ensuring each show was a unique experience. This not only revitalized their performances but also fostered a sense of camaraderie within the EDM community.

A Focus on Authenticity

Throughout their rebirth, Krewella remained steadfast in their commitment to authenticity. They shared their struggles, vulnerabilities, and triumphs with their fans, inviting them into their journey of growth and self-discovery. This transparency not only strengthened their connection with their audience but also inspired others to embrace their own authenticity.

Krewella's authenticity extended beyond their music. They became vocal advocates for causes they believed in, using their platform to raise awareness about social issues and promote positive change. Their genuine commitment to making a difference resonated with fans worldwide and cemented their status as more than just musicians.

The Rebirth Unleashed

The culmination of Krewella's rebirth was the release of their highly anticipated album, "Amplify." This collection of tracks served as a testament to their transformation, showcasing their evolution both sonically and personally. Each song took listeners on a journey, exploring themes of resilience, self-empowerment, and the beauty of embracing change.

"Amplify" debuted at the top of the charts, proving that Krewella's rebirth had struck a powerful chord with fans and critics alike. It was a resounding success not just because of the numbers but also because it represented the culmination of years of growth, perseverance, and the unwavering belief in their art.

The Unconventional Path to Rebirth

Krewella's rebirth was not without its challenges, and the path they took was far from conventional. They defied industry norms and broke free from the confines of a traditional musical journey. Instead, they forged their own path, facing adversity head-on and coming out stronger than ever.

In the face of criticism and doubt, Krewella stood tall, remaining true to themselves and their music. Their story serves as a source of inspiration for aspiring artists, reminding them that setbacks and failures are not the end but rather opportunities for growth and reinvention.

Lessons for the Modern Artist

Krewella's journey of rebirth holds valuable lessons for the modern artist. It emphasizes the importance of staying true to one's vision, even in the face of adversity. It encourages artists to embrace change, push boundaries, and continuously evolve in their craft.

Furthermore, Krewella's story highlights the power of connection and collaboration. By opening themselves up to new ideas and perspectives, artists can tap into a wellspring of creativity and reach new levels of success.

In a music industry that often prioritizes commercial success over artistic integrity, Krewella's rebirth is a testament to the enduring power of authenticity. It serves as a beacon of hope for artists navigating the tumultuous waters of the music industry, reminding them that their voice and creative vision are worth fighting for.

Exercises for Rebirth

1. Write a reflective journal entry about a personal setback or failure that you have experienced in your creative journey. Explore how it has shaped you and identify opportunities for growth and rebirth.

2. Experiment with blending different genres in your own music or art. Take inspiration from Krewella's exploration of different styles and find new ways to express yourself creatively.

3. Reach out to another artist or creative professional for a collaboration. Embrace the opportunity to learn from each other and create something unique together.

4. Use your platform, no matter how big or small, to advocate for a cause or issue that is important to you. Share your authentic voice and encourage others to join you in making a positive impact.

5. Create a vision board or collage that represents your personal rebirth. Include images, quotes, and symbols that capture your growth and aspirations as an artist.

Remember, the journey of rebirth is a deeply personal and transformative one. Embrace the challenges, take risks, and let your true self shine through in your creative endeavors. The world is waiting for your rebirth.

Redemption and Reconnection

In the face of personal and professional challenges, Krewella found redemption and reconnection that would propel them forward in their music career. This chapter explores their journey of growth, resilience, and ultimately, finding their place in the world of music.

The Price of Fame

As Krewella gained popularity, they faced the harsh reality of fame and its consequences. The pressures to maintain success and meet the expectations of their fans took a toll on the sisters' mental and emotional well-being. They found themselves battling insecurities and succumbing to the negative influences of the industry. It seemed as though the limelight was tearing them apart rather than bringing them closer.

The Pressure to Perform

One major challenge they encountered was the pressure to constantly perform at their best. The demanding schedules, late nights, and non-stop traveling began to take a toll on their physical and mental health. Burnout became a real threat, and their artistic creativity suffered as a result.

Personal Struggles and Addiction

Amidst the chaos of their growing stardom, personal struggles haunted both Jahan and Yasmine. They found solace in unhealthy coping mechanisms, leading to addiction and self-destructive behaviors. This tumultuous period in their lives put a strain on their relationship as sisters and bandmates.

Turbulent Relationships Within the Group

The bond between Jahan and Yasmine was tested during this challenging time. Miscommunications, disagreements, and different visions for the future of Krewella strained their relationships. The once unbreakable bond began to weaken, and they felt lost in the midst of their individual journeys.

Krewella's Unbreakable Bond

Despite their struggles, the sisters refused to let go of their deep connection. Recognizing the importance of their relationship, they made efforts to rebuild trust, communicate openly, and support each other through the darkest of times. This commitment to their sisterhood would be instrumental in their redemption and reconnection.

A New Direction and Creative Evolution

To find their way back to each other, Krewella decided to take a step back from the relentless touring and spotlight. They took the time to reflect on their experiences, dig deep within themselves, and rediscover their passion for music. This period of introspection marked the beginning of a new chapter for Krewella.

Collaborations and Experimentations

During their hiatus, Jahan and Yasmine explored various collaborations and experimental projects. They worked with different artists from diverse genres, challenging themselves to step outside of their comfort zone and expand their musical horizons. These experiences opened up new possibilities and allowed them to reinvent their sound.

The Release of "Ammunition EP"

In 2016, Krewella returned with a powerful statement through the release of their highly anticipated "Ammunition EP." This collection of tracks showcased their growth as artists and their resilience in the face of adversity. The EP received critical acclaim and resonated with their dedicated fan base, solidifying their redemption in the eyes of both the music industry and their audience.

The Rebirth of Krewella

With their redemption came a renewed sense of purpose and determination. Krewella emerged from their struggles stronger than ever, embracing their individuality and the unique dynamic they brought to the music scene. They owned their past, learning from their mistakes and using them as fuel for their creative fire.

Redemption and Reconnection

In their journey towards redemption, Jahan and Yasmine not only found solace in their sisterly bond but also realized the importance of reconnecting with their fans. They reached out in vulnerability, sharing their stories and struggles through their music and social media platforms. This authenticity allowed them to rebuild trust and form a deeper connection with their audience.

Through their story of redemption and reconnection, Krewella reminds us that setbacks and challenges can be opportunities for growth. Their resilience and commitment to their artistry serve as an inspiration to anyone facing adversity, encouraging them to find redemption in their own lives.

The Legacy of Neon Frequencies

Neon Frequencies, the journey of Krewella, has left an indelible mark on the music industry. Their unique sound and fearless approach to pushing boundaries have inspired a new generation of artists. Their legacy lives on not only in their music but also in their activism and philanthropic efforts.

Krewella in Today's Music Scene

In today's music scene, Krewella continues to evolve and redefine what it means to be an electronic music duo. They have continued to release music that resonates with their fan base and have consistently pushed the envelope with their live performances. Their energy and passion remain unmatched, ensuring their relevance in the ever-changing music landscape.

The Future of Neon Frequencies

As Krewella looks towards the future, they remain committed to their artistic growth and connection with their fans. The journey of Neon Frequencies is far from over, as Jahan and Yasmine continue to explore new sounds, collaborate with other artists, and challenge the boundaries of electronic dance music. With redemption and reconnection as their guiding principles, the future holds endless possibilities for Krewella and their ever-growing fan base.

Chapter Four: Going Global

From Local to International

Conquering Festivals Worldwide

The journey of Krewella from a local act to an international sensation can be traced through their unstoppable conquest of festivals worldwide. These events served as the perfect stage for Jahan and Yasmine to showcase their unique sound, electrifying performances, and captivating energy to a diverse audience.

The Festival Scene: A Global Phenomenon

Over the past few decades, music festivals have evolved into a global phenomenon, attracting millions of music lovers from all corners of the world. These immersive experiences offer a unique blend of music, art, culture, and community, creating a vibrant atmosphere that transcends geographical boundaries.

From the legendary Woodstock festival in the 1960s to the present-day Coachella Valley Music and Arts Festival, festivals have become a pivotal platform for artists to connect with their fans on a massive scale. They not only provide a platform to showcase their talent and artistry but also offer an opportunity to break through to new audiences and leave a lasting impact.

Krewella's Festival Odyssey

Krewella quickly recognized the power of music festivals and realized that these events were the perfect arena to unleash their electrifying performances and connect with a diverse audience. Jahan and Yasmine ventured into the festival scene and left an indelible mark with their infectious energy, dynamic stage presence, and genre-defying music.

Their festival odyssey began with smaller local events in the vibrant city of Chicago, where they developed a loyal following. The sisters' fiery performances and their ability to seamlessly fuse different musical genres set them apart from the crowd, gaining attention from festival organizers and fellow artists.

As their reputation grew, Krewella started receiving invitations to perform at larger festivals across the United States. From Electric Daisy Carnival (EDC) to Ultra Music Festival, their powerful performances left festival-goers craving more.

Crafting Unforgettable Moments

Krewella's ability to create unforgettable moments was a testament to their dedication and passion for their craft. Their festival performances were carefully curated experiences, aimed at creating a connection with their audience and leaving a lasting impression.

The sisters understood that festivals were not just about playing their popular hits but also about curating a set that takes the crowd on a musical journey. They showcased their versatility by seamlessly blending different genres, including electronic dance music, pop, rock, and hip-hop, captivating audiences with their diverse soundscapes.

One of the defining moments of their festival journey was their performance at Tomorrowland, one of the largest electronic music festivals in the world. Krewella took the stage by storm, delivering an electrifying performance that combined their signature high-energy sound with visually stunning production elements. The infectious energy radiating from the crowd was a testament to their ability to connect with fans on a global scale.

Leveraging Technology and Innovation

Krewella's success in conquering festivals worldwide can also be attributed to their embrace of technology and innovation. They recognized the power of social media platforms and used them to promote their festival appearances, engage with fans, and create anticipation for their performances.

Additionally, the sisters embraced emerging technologies to enhance their live shows. From incorporating cutting-edge visual effects and lighting design to integrating live instrumentation and vocal performances, Krewella pushed the boundaries of what a traditional DJ set could be. They seamlessly blended live elements with electronic production, creating a truly immersive and unforgettable experience for festival-goers.

Empowering the Crowd

What made Krewella's festival performances truly exceptional was their ability to empower the crowd. Their infectious energy and genuine connection with their fans created a sense of unity and empowerment within the crowd.

During their performances, Jahan and Yasmine encouraged festival-goers to let go of their inhibitions, embrace the present moment, and celebrate the power of music. Their performances became a platform for self-expression, where fans from all walks of life could come together, dance, and celebrate their shared love for music.

Conclusion

Krewella's unparalleled success in conquering festivals worldwide can be attributed to their unrelenting passion, captivating performances, and their ability to connect with fans on a deep level. The festival scene served as a transformative platform for the sisters, allowing them to showcase their unique sound, push boundaries, and inspire a new generation of artists.

Their festival journey was not just about performing on stage; it was about creating unforgettable moments, empowering the crowd, and leaving a lasting impact in the hearts and minds of their fans. Krewella's legacy in the festival scene will forever be etched in the annals of electronic dance music history, serving as an inspiration for aspiring artists to follow their dreams and conquer the world, one festival at a time.

The Power of Live Performances

One of the defining features of Krewella's success has been their electrifying live performances. From the very beginning, Jahan and Yasmine understood the importance of captivating their audience and creating an unforgettable experience. They recognized that in the world of Electronic Dance Music (EDM), a live show could be a game-changer. In this section, we will explore the power of Krewella's live performances and how they have solidified their place in the music industry.

Creating an Immersive Atmosphere

A Krewella concert is not just a show, it is a full-blown experience that takes the audience on a journey. The sisters have a unique ability to create an immersive atmosphere through their music, visuals, and stage presence. They understand that a live performance is not just about the music, but about the overall experience.

To achieve this, Krewella combines their high-energy tracks with stunning visuals and stage design. They incorporate vibrant LED screens, lasers, and pyrotechnics to enhance the visual impact of their shows. The combination of lights, visuals, and music creates an otherworldly atmosphere that transports the audience into Krewella's world.

Engaging with the Crowd

Krewella's live performances are not just a one-way street. They actively engage with the crowd, making every concert feel personal and intimate. Jahan and Yasmine have a natural charisma that allows them to connect with their fans on a deep level.

During their shows, they frequently interact with the audience, whether it's through shoutouts, encouraging crowd participation, or even jumping into the crowd. By breaking down the barrier between the stage and the audience, Krewella creates a sense of unity and inclusivity that is hard to replicate.

Energy and Passion

One of the most striking aspects of Krewella's live performances is their boundless energy and passion. Jahan and Yasmine give every ounce of themselves on stage, leaving the audience in awe of their dedication and love for what they do.

Their infectious energy is contagious, spreading throughout the crowd and fueling a sense of collective euphoria. Krewella shows are known for their high-intensity moments, where the sisters and their fans are completely immersed in the music.

Improvisation and Live Remixing

Krewella's live performances are anything but scripted. They thrive on improvisation and live remixing, creating a unique experience for each show. Jahan is responsible for live vocals, often adding her own spin to the songs, while Yasmine takes control of the energy on stage as she mixes and transitions between tracks.

This element of unpredictability keeps the audience engaged and excited, as they never know what surprise Krewella has in store for them. It also showcases the sisters' immense talent and versatility as musicians.

The Ripple Effect

The impact of Krewella's live performances extends far beyond the concert venue. Their shows have a ripple effect that resonates with their fans long after the music stops. The energy, emotions, and memories created during a Krewella concert stay with the audience, becoming a part of their personal journey.

Fans often describe Krewella shows as transformative experiences that have helped them overcome obstacles, find strength, and embrace their individuality. Through the power of their live performances, Jahan and Yasmine have touched the lives of countless people around the world.

Conclusion

In the world of EDM, live performances can make or break an artist's career. Krewella's ability to captivate audiences through their immersive atmosphere, crowd engagement, energy, and passion has cemented their status as one of the most influential acts in the industry.

Their live shows are more than just entertainment; they are transformative experiences that bring people together, spark emotions, and create lasting memories. The power of Krewella's live performances lies not only in their music but also in the connection they foster with their fans.

As they continue to evolve and push boundaries, Krewella's live performances will undoubtedly remain a driving force behind their enduring legacy in the music world. Their ability to create an unforgettable experience will continue to inspire and impact the EDM community for years to come.

International Success and Fan Base

Ah, international success and a devoted fan base - every artist's dream come true! And Krewella knows all about it. From the local Chicago scene to conquering stages across the globe, the Krewella sisters have built a dedicated following that spans borders and transcends cultural boundaries.

When Krewella burst onto the EDM scene, they quickly caught the attention of music lovers around the world. Their unique sound, blending elements of pop, rock, and electronic music, struck a chord with listeners everywhere. But it wasn't just their music that resonated with fans - it was their energy, their passion, and their authenticity.

As Jahan and Yasmine traveled from city to city, country to country, they witnessed the power of their music firsthand. Their live performances became legendary, as they unleashed an electrifying energy that infected audiences with an irresistible desire to dance and let loose. It was a shared experience, a collective moment of euphoria, that created an unbreakable bond between Krewella and their fans.

And it wasn't just the Krewella sisters' music that captivated international audiences. Their message of female empowerment, self-expression, and pushing boundaries struck a chord with fans all over the world. In an industry dominated by male artists, Krewella fearlessly carved out their space, proving that women could be at the top of their game.

Their international success didn't come without its fair share of challenges, though. Touring across different time zones, dealing with language barriers, and navigating unfamiliar cultures posed their own set of obstacles. But true to their resilient nature, Jahan and Yasmine embraced these challenges head-on, transforming them into opportunities for growth and connection.

Social media played a crucial role in Krewella's global reach. As fans eagerly clicked "follow," "like," and "share," the Krewella sisters harnessed the power of social platforms to connect with their fan base on a personal level. They shared glimpses into their lives, behind-the-scenes moments, and intimate stories that allowed fans to see the people behind the music.

But it wasn't just the virtual world where Krewella made an impact. Festivals became their playground, and Krewella set out to conquer them all. From Ultra Music Festival in Miami to Tomorrowland in Belgium, their electrifying performances and infectious energy turned every stage into a pulsating sea of fans. The roar of the crowd, the flashing lights, the shared experience of music - it was pure magic.

Krewella's international success and fan base also fueled their journey as philanthropists. They recognized the power of their platform and used it to support causes close to their hearts. From raising awareness about mental health to advocating for LGBTQ+ rights, Krewella became champions of change, inspiring their fan base to stand up for what they believe in.

But what truly makes Krewella's fan base unique is the depth of their connection. It's not just about the music; it's about the shared experiences, the personal stories, and the belief in something greater. Krewella's fans, known as "Krew," are a diverse community that spans continents and cultures, united by their love for the music and the message.

The international success and fan base that Krewella has earned are a testament to their talent, their authenticity, and their unwavering dedication. They have become a beacon of light in the EDM world, inspiring countless artists to follow their dreams and embrace their true selves.

And as Krewella continues to push boundaries and chart new territories, their fan base will be there every step of the way, cheering them on, and dancing to the beat of their music. Together, Krewella and their fans are rewriting the rules, creating a vibrant and inclusive community that celebrates the power of music and the strength of unity.

So, join the Krew and let the neon frequencies guide you on an electrifying journey of music, empowerment, and unforgettable moments. Because with Krewella, the party is just getting started.

Touring Adventures and Misadventures

Touring is an exhilarating experience for any band, providing them with the opportunity to connect with fans on a personal level and showcase their music to a wider audience. For Krewella, touring has been a series of incredible adventures and unpredictable misadventures that have shaped their journey and made it all the more memorable.

The Opening Act: Small Venues, Big Dreams

When Krewella first began touring, they started small, playing in intimate venues and clubs that could hold only a few hundred people. These early shows were characterized by a raw energy and an intense connection with the audience. Jahan and Yasmine, known for their high-energy performances, would leave everything on the stage, creating an electric atmosphere that left the crowd craving for more.

The Road Warriors: From Coast to Coast

As Krewella's popularity grew, so did their tour schedule. They went from playing small gigs in Chicago to embarking on nationwide tours, bringing their unique sound to fans all across the United States. Their relentless work ethic and dedication to their craft earned them the title of "Road Warriors." From coast to coast, Krewella would travel in cramped tour buses, overcoming fatigue and pushing their boundaries to deliver unforgettable performances night after night.

Unexpected Adventures and Hilarious Mishaps

Life on the road is never without its fair share of unexpected adventures and hilarious mishaps, and Krewella has had their fair share of stories to tell. Whether it's getting lost in unfamiliar cities, dealing with temperamental equipment, or surviving on nothing but fast food, the sisters have experienced it all. These misadventures have often led to bonding moments and inside jokes within the band, creating lifelong memories and strengthening their bond as sisters and bandmates.

Cultural Immersion: Exploring the World Through Music

Touring has also given Krewella the unique opportunity to explore different cultures and immerse themselves in the local music scenes of various countries. From the bustling streets of Tokyo to the vibrant nightlife of Ibiza, they have embraced the world as their stage. Collaborating with local artists and learning about different music traditions has enriched their sound and helped them grow as musicians.

From Highlight Reels to Horror Stories: The Emotional Rollercoaster

While touring is undoubtedly an incredible and fulfilling experience, there are also moments of exhaustion, homesickness, and emotional highs and lows. Late nights, constant traveling, and being away from loved ones can take a toll on even the most resilient performers. Krewella has experienced these challenges firsthand. However, they have always managed to find strength in each other and in the love and support of their fans.

Changing Lives, One Show at a Time

Despite the challenges, Krewella's touring adventures have brought them immense joy and fulfillment. They have witnessed firsthand the impact their music has on the lives of their fans. The power to bring people together and create unforgettable moments is what drives them to continue spreading their message of love, unity, and self-expression.

Unconventional Wisdom: Embracing Spontaneity

One of the defining characteristics of Krewella's touring adventures is their ability to embrace spontaneity. Whether it's impromptu acoustic sets in unexpected locations or surprise collaborations with fellow artists, they thrive on the thrill of the unknown. By embracing the unexpected, Krewella has been able to push their creative boundaries and create even more magical moments on stage.

The Ultimate Fan Experience: VIP Meet and Greets

One of the perks of touring is the opportunity to connect with fans in a more intimate setting. Krewella has always prioritized their fans and makes it a point to offer VIP meet and greets at their shows. These exclusive experiences allow fans to have a personal interaction with the band, take photos, and even receive autographs. It's a chance for Krewella to express their gratitude for the unwavering support of their fans.

The Show Must Go On: Triumphs in the Face of Adversity

No touring adventure would be complete without a few hiccups along the way. From technical difficulties to last-minute venue changes, Krewella has faced their fair share of challenges on the road. But true to their resilient nature, they have always found a way to overcome these obstacles and deliver unforgettable performances. The show must go on, and Krewella's determination and passion have ensured that it always does.

In the whirlwind of touring adventures and misadventures, Krewella has continuously grown and evolved as artists. Each experience on the road has shaped them and allowed them to connect with their fans in a profound way. As they continue to spread their infectious energy and uplifting music worldwide, their touring adventures will forever be a testament to their unwavering dedication and unbreakable bond as Neon Frequencies.

Expanding Krewella's Sound and Style

When it comes to expanding their sound and style, Krewella is no stranger to pushing the boundaries of the electronic dance music (EDM) genre. Jahan and Yasmine, the dynamic duo behind the band, have continually evolved their music, incorporating diverse influences and experimenting with new techniques. In this section, we will explore how Krewella has expanded their sound and style, forging a unique path in the music industry.

Incorporating Different Genres

One of the key ways in which Krewella has expanded their sound is by incorporating elements from different genres into their music. They have never been afraid to blend various styles, creating a fusion that is distinctly their own. From dance-pop to dubstep, trap to rock, Krewella has masterfully crafted a sound that transcends traditional EDM boundaries.

Take their hit song "Alive" for example. Released in 2012, it seamlessly combines elements of electronic music with powerful pop-infused vocals. The catchy melody and infectious energy attracted a wide range of listeners, bridging the gap between EDM and mainstream pop.

Exploring New Production Techniques

In addition to experimenting with different genres, Krewella has always been at the forefront of exploring new production techniques. They have consistently pushed the limits of what is possible within the EDM realm, incorporating unconventional sounds and intricate layers into their music.

For instance, in their track "Killin' It," released in 2012, they introduced a heavy dubstep bassline accompanied by energetic synths and glitchy effects. This unique combination of elements created a distinctive sound that set them apart from their contemporaries.

Collaborating with Diverse Artists

Krewella's commitment to expanding their sound is also evident through their collaborations with diverse artists. They have worked with both established musicians and up-and-coming talents, bringing fresh perspectives to their music.

One notable collaboration is their work with the Dutch DJ and producer, Tiësto, on the song "Set Yourself Free." Released in 2014, this track showcased Krewella's ability to seamlessly blend their signature sound with Tiësto's progressive house style. The result was a powerful and anthemic dancefloor banger that resonated with fans worldwide.

Incorporating Live Instruments

Another aspect that sets Krewella apart is their incorporation of live instruments into their performances and recordings. Alongside their electronic production, Jahan and Yasmine have skillfully integrated live instruments such as guitars, drums, and even violins into their music.

In their song "Enjoy the Ride," released in 2013, they combined electronic beats with the raw energy of live drums, creating an electrifying and dynamic fusion that captivated audiences. This unique blend of electronic and live instruments added an extra layer of depth and authenticity to their sound.

Experimenting with Vocal Techniques

Krewella's exploration of sound extends beyond instrumentation and production techniques. They have also pushed the boundaries of vocal techniques, experimenting with different styles and effects.

In their track "Somewhere to Run," released in 2015, Jahan and Yasmine showcased their versatility as vocalists by utilizing a mixture of powerful harmonies, modulated vocal effects, and emotive delivery. This experimentation added a unique sonic dimension to their music, amplifying the emotional impact of their songs.

Creating an Immersive Visual Experience

Expanding their sound and style goes beyond just the music for Krewella. They have also crafted an immersive visual experience to complement their live performances. From their striking stage setups to their captivating music videos, Krewella has always been attentive to the visual aspect of their art.

For example, in their music video for "Alive," they incorporated vibrant and dynamic visuals that mirrored the energy of the song. This attention to detail created a multi-sensory experience that enhanced their overall artistic vision.

A Contemporary Challenge

As Krewella continues to explore new territory and expand their sound and style, one of the contemporary challenges they face is the need to balance innovation with maintaining their distinctive identity. While it is important to evolve and adapt to the ever-changing music landscape, it is equally crucial for them to stay true to their unique sound that initially catapulted them to success.

To navigate this challenge, Krewella must continuously push themselves creatively while remaining authentic to their artistic vision. This involves experimenting with new techniques, collaborating with diverse artists, and staying connected to their fan base to gauge their preferences and expectations.

Ultimately, Krewella's ability to expand their sound and style lies in their willingness to take risks, embrace new influences, and continually reinvent themselves. By staying true to their passion for music and their fans, they will undoubtedly continue to leave an indelible mark on the EDM scene.

So, as Krewella moves forward on their musical journey, they will undoubtedly blaze new trails and continue to expand their sound and style, delighting listeners around the world with their inventive and captivating music.

The Release of "New World Pt. 1"

As Krewella continued to evolve and experiment with their sound, they embarked on a new musical journey with the highly anticipated release of their EP, "New World Pt. 1". This release marked a significant milestone in their career, showcasing their growth as artists and their ability to push the boundaries of electronic dance music.

The inspiration behind "New World Pt. 1" came from Krewella's desire to explore new sonic territories and create a body of work that would resonate with their fans on a deeper level. This EP represented a departure from their previous releases, incorporating a diverse range of musical elements and genre influences.

One of the standout tracks on "New World Pt. 1" is "Be There", a collaboration with Canadian producer Diskord. This high-energy track seamlessly blends elements of trap music with Krewella's signature melodic vocals, creating a powerful and addictive anthem that quickly captivated listeners. With its infectious hooks and hard-hitting beats, "Be There" became an instant fan favorite and solidified Krewella's position as innovators in the EDM scene.

Another standout track on the EP is "Parachute," a collaboration with Canadian producer Justin Caruso. This emotionally charged song showcases the sisters' vulnerable side, with introspective lyrics and a beautifully layered production. The combination of Jahan and Yasmine's heartfelt vocals, heartfelt lyrics, and Caruso's masterful production create a truly captivating and moving listening experience.

In addition to these collaborations, "New World Pt. 1" features a collection of solo tracks that highlight Krewella's individual strengths as artists. From the anthemic "Be There" to the introspective and emotionally charged "Parachute," each song on the EP offers a unique glimpse into Krewella's creative evolution.

With the release of "New World Pt. 1," Krewella once again demonstrated their ability to push the boundaries of EDM and deliver a fresh and innovative sound. The EP received widespread critical acclaim and further solidified their position as one of the industry's most exciting and forward-thinking acts.

Not only did "New World Pt. 1" resonate with fans, but it also garnered the attention of music industry insiders. The EP quickly climbed the charts, reaching the top spots on various EDM charts and further cementing Krewella's status as a top-tier act. The success of "New World Pt. 1" also led to an increased demand for live performances, with the sisters embarking on a highly successful tour to promote the EP.

Despite their success, Krewella remained humble and grounded throughout the release of "New World Pt. 1." They took the time to connect with their fans, expressing their gratitude for their continued support and sharing behind-the-scenes stories of the creative process behind the EP. This personal connection with their audience further endeared them to their dedicated fan base, solidifying their position as not just musicians, but as relatable and authentic individuals.

As Krewella continues to push the boundaries of EDM, their release of "New World Pt. 1" serves as a testament to their artistic growth and unwavering dedication to their craft. With its diverse range of musical styles and captivating production, this EP marks a new chapter in Krewella's musical journey, propelling them even further into the global music scene.

Aspiring musicians can learn from Krewella's ability to reinvent themselves and explore new musical horizons. By remaining true to their artistic vision and embracing creativity, Krewella continues to inspire a new generation of artists to break free from genre constraints and carve their own paths in the music industry.

With the release of "New World Pt. 1," Krewella solidified their reputation as pioneers in electronic dance music and further established their enduring legacy as artists who push the boundaries of what is possible in the genre. Their unyielding passion and relentless pursuit of musical excellence continue to inspire and captivate audiences around the world.

Resources and References

1. Park, J. (2017). "Krewella showcases artistic growth with 'New World Pt. 1.'" *EDM Identity*. Retrieved from: https://edmidentity.com/2017/06/08/krewella-new-world-pt1/

2. Sweeney, F. (2017). "Krewella releases new 'New World Pt. 1' EP, featuring collaborations with Diskord, Pegboard Nerds, and more." *Dancing Astronaut*. Retrieved from: https://dancingastronaut.com/2017/06/krewella-releases-new-world-pt-1-ep-featuring-collaborations-

3. Wass, M. (2017). "Krewella's 'New World Pt. 1' is another chapter in their pop-focused evolution." *Idolator*. Retrieved from: https://www.idolator.com/7661112/krewella-interview-marshmello-adventure-club?view-all

Breaking Barriers: A Female-Dominated Industry

In the male-dominated music industry, Krewella's rise to fame as a female electronic dance music (EDM) group was nothing short of groundbreaking. Jahan and Yasmine, the Krewella sisters, defied all odds and shattered barriers, paving the way for women in a genre that had largely been dominated by men. Their fearless pursuit of their dreams and unapologetic expression of their talent has inspired a new generation of female artists to break free from societal norms and make their mark in the industry.

Challenging the Status Quo

When Krewella burst onto the scene, it was apparent that they were not just another girl group. Their infectious beats, powerful vocals, and electrifying performances commanded attention and demanded respect. They didn't conform to the industry's expectations of what a female artist should be; instead, they fearlessly embraced their individuality and carved their own path.

Empowering Women in the EDM Community

Krewella's success in a male-dominated industry didn't just stop at their own achievements; they actively worked to empower women in the EDM community. Through their music, they encouraged women to pursue their dreams and not be limited by societal boundaries. Their message of empowerment resonated with fans across the world, inspiring them to step out of their comfort zones and unleash their true potential.

Championing Diversity and Inclusivity

Krewella's impact extended beyond gender barriers. They championed diversity and inclusivity, celebrating people from all walks of life. With their fusion of different genres and styles, they brought together a diverse fan base, breaking down the walls that divided music lovers. Their music became a platform for unity and acceptance, proving that music has the power to bring people together regardless of their differences.

Overcoming Stereotypes and Prejudices

As pioneers in the EDM industry, Krewella faced their fair share of stereotypes and prejudices. Critics questioned their credibility and dismissed their success as a result of marketing tactics rather than talent. However, Jahan and Yasmine remained unshaken, using their music as a vessel to prove their worth. Their relentless dedication, combined with their undeniable talent, silenced the naysayers and solidified their rightful place in the industry.

Inspiring Future Generations

Krewella's impact on future generations of female artists cannot be overstated. They shattered the glass ceiling, showing aspiring musicians that their dreams are within reach. The Krewella sisters became role models for young women, proving that hard work, determination, and a refusal to conform can lead to extraordinary success.

Changing the Narrative of Success

Krewella's success not only challenged gender norms but also changed the narrative of success in the music industry. They proved that talent and creativity are the true markers of achievement, regardless of gender. Their rise to stardom showcased that women can achieve greatness in EDM and any other genre they choose to pursue.

A Platform for Social Change

Krewella didn't just use their musical platform to entertain; they used it to advocate for social change as well. They addressed important issues such as gender inequality, mental health, and societal pressures in their lyrics, sparking conversations and raising awareness. By merging activism with their music, they demonstrated the transformative power of art and its ability to inspire social change.

Continuing the Journey

While Krewella's journey has been one of triumph and breaking barriers, their work is far from over. As they continue to navigate the ever-evolving music industry, they remain committed to pushing boundaries and empowering the voices of women. Their legacy as pioneers of a female-dominated industry will inspire generations to come, reminding them that anything is possible when passion and talent collide.

Through their unwavering determination, Krewella has shattered the glass ceiling, proving that women have an indelible place in the world of EDM. Breaking through the barriers of a male-dominated industry, they have opened doors for future generations of female artists, encouraging them to embrace their uniqueness and pursue their dreams fearlessly. Krewella's success is not just a story of triumph; it is a testament to the power of resilience and the undeniable talent that knows no boundaries. They have redefined what it means to be a female artist in the EDM community, leaving an enduring legacy that will continue to inspire and empower women across the globe.

The Power of Female Empowerment

The power of female empowerment is a driving force behind the success and influence of Krewella. Jahan and Yasmine, the Krewella sisters, have shattered traditional gender norms in the male-dominated music industry, inspiring women around the world to pursue their passions and break barriers.

In this section, we will explore the impact of female empowerment in the context of Krewella's journey, highlighting their accomplishments, challenges, and contributions to gender equality.

Addressing Gender Imbalances

The music industry has long been plagued by gender disparities, with women facing obstacles and marginalization. However, Krewella has fearlessly challenged these imbalances from the start.

The Krewella sisters broke into the electronic dance music (EDM) scene, asserting their unique voice and style. They refused to conform to the industry's expectations and carved their own path, empowering countless women to do the same.

Inspiration and Representation

Krewella's rise to prominence has served as a source of inspiration and representation for women in music. By sharing their story, struggles, and triumphs, they have given a voice to those who have been silenced and marginalized.

Their success offers a beacon of hope to aspiring female artists, encouraging them to pursue their dreams and not be limited by societal norms or gender biases.

Breaking Stereotypes

Krewella's unapologetically bold and daring persona has shattered stereotypes within the EDM community. They have shown that femininity and strength are not mutually exclusive and that women can dominate traditionally male-dominated spaces.

Through their music and performances, Krewella challenges the notion that women should be confined to certain roles or genres. They embrace their femininity while asserting their authority, dismantling societal expectations and empowering women to embrace their authentic selves.

Advocacy for Women's Rights

Krewella's advocacy extends beyond the music industry. They actively engage in social and political activism, championing causes such as women's rights and gender equality.

By using their platform to raise awareness and support initiatives that promote women's empowerment, Krewella demonstrates the power of music as a catalyst for change. Their boldness and dedication to social justice inspire their fans to take action and fight for a more inclusive and equal world.

Philanthropy and Giving Back

In addition to their advocacy work, Krewella has demonstrated their commitment to giving back. They have engaged in numerous philanthropic efforts, supporting various causes such as education, healthcare, and disaster relief.

Through their philanthropy, Krewella showcases the importance of using success and influence to uplift others. Their generosity and dedication to making a positive impact further amplify their message of empowerment.

Supporting Women in the Industry

Krewella actively supports and uplifts fellow female artists, recognizing the importance of solidarity and collaboration. They have collaborated with and mentored emerging talent, providing opportunities and guidance to aspiring women in the industry.

By dedicating themselves to supporting other women, Krewella creates a network of empowerment, fostering a sense of community and strength.

Redefined Success and Influence

Krewella's success and influence go beyond music sales and chart rankings. They have redefined what it means to be successful, emphasizing the importance of authenticity, empowerment, and social impact.

Their ability to connect with fans on a deep and personal level has been instrumental in their influence. Through their music and message, Krewella encourages their audience to embrace their uniqueness, challenge societal norms, and strive for personal and societal growth.

Looking Ahead

As Krewella continues to evolve and inspire, their commitment to female empowerment remains unwavering. Their influence will continue to shape the music industry and inspire future generations of artists.

With their determination, resilience, and passion, Krewella paves the way for a future where gender equality is the norm, and women in music are celebrated, respected, and empowered.

Conclusion

The power of female empowerment is at the core of Krewella's success and legacy. Through their music, advocacy, and philanthropy, they have shattered gender barriers, inspired women, and pushed for a more inclusive and equal industry.

Krewella's story serves as a reminder of the immense potential for change that lies within music and the arts. They have shown that, with passion, perseverance, and a commitment to empowering others, anyone can make a profound impact and create a more equitable world.

The Legacy of Neon Frequencies

The legacy of Neon Frequencies, the band formed by the Krewella sisters Jahan and Yasmine, represents a groundbreaking phenomenon in the world of electronic dance music (EDM) and leaves a lasting impact on the music industry. From their innovative sound to their trailblazing activism, Krewella's legacy is a testament to their talent, resilience, and determination to break barriers and inspire others.

Pioneers of Electronic Dance Music

Krewella emerged during the rise of EDM in the early 2010s, and they quickly became pioneers of the genre. Their unique blend of melodic hooks, heavy beats, and emotionally charged lyrics set them apart from the rest, capturing the attention of both mainstream audiences and avid EDM fans. Their debut album, "Get Wet," showcased their ability to push boundaries and redefine electronic music.

The legacy of Neon Frequencies lies in their ability to bridge the gap between electronic music and other genres, infusing elements of pop, rock, and hip-hop into their tracks. Their experimental approach and incorporation of live instruments revolutionized EDM, opening the door for a new era of electronic music.

Breaking Stereotypes and Pushing Boundaries

Beyond their musical contributions, Krewella shattered stereotypes within the industry. As females in a male-dominated field, Jahan and Yasmine defied expectations and proved that talent knows no gender. Their success challenged the notion that women are merely vocalists or eye candy in the world of EDM, inspiring a new generation of female artists to pursue their dreams fearlessly.

Krewella's legacy lies in their unwavering commitment to pushing boundaries and defying norms. They broke free from the constraints of traditional EDM, experimenting with diverse sounds and incorporating thought-provoking lyrics.

Their fearlessness in exploring new territories transformed the genre and empowered others to think outside the box.

Inspiring a New Generation of Artists

One of the most significant aspects of Krewella's legacy is their ability to inspire a new generation of artists. Through their journey, they demonstrated the importance of staying true to oneself and embracing individuality. Their relentless pursuit of their passion and dedication to their craft serve as a blueprint for aspiring musicians, reminding them that success is possible with hard work and authenticity.

Krewella's impact extends beyond their music; through their openness about their personal struggles, they have become a guiding light for individuals facing their battles. Their willingness to speak openly about addiction and mental health issues has led to a greater conversation within the music industry, encouraging artists and fans alike to seek help and support.

Political and Social Activism

Neon Frequencies stands as an example of the power of music as a platform for political and social activism. Krewella has utilized their influence to champion causes close to their hearts, from LGBTQ+ rights to environmental conservation. By lending their voices to these important issues, they have brought awareness and sparked conversations, encouraging their fans to engage with the world around them.

Their philanthropic efforts include partnering with organizations like Dance For Paralysis, advocating for spinal cord injury research and awareness. Krewella's legacy lies in their dedication to making a difference, using their success as a means to create positive change.

The Enduring Legacy of Neon Frequencies

Krewella's journey, filled with triumphs and challenges, leaves behind an enduring legacy. Their innovative sound, fearlessness in pushing boundaries, and commitment to inspiring others have forever shaped the EDM landscape. The impact of Neon Frequencies can be felt not only through their music, but also through their activism and unwavering spirit.

Their story serves as a testament to the power of sisterhood, resilience, and the pursuit of one's passion. Their legacy lives on as an inspiration to musicians, creators, and dreamers around the world, reminding us all to embrace our unique voices and strive for greatness.

In the words of Krewella themselves, "The power that lies within music is astounding, and it is a universal language that connects us all. May the legacy of Neon Frequencies continue to inspire and uplift, reminding us of the transformative power of music."

Chapter Five: Krewella's Impact

The Influence of Krewella

Chapter Five: Krewella's Impact

Pioneers of Electronic Dance Music

Electronic Dance Music (EDM) has become one of the most popular and influential genres in the contemporary music scene. With its infectious beats, pulsating rhythms, and energetic live performances, EDM has taken the world by storm. And at the forefront of this global movement are the talented sisters Jahan and Yasmine, better known as Krewella.

The Birth of a Musical Revolution

Krewella burst onto the music scene with their unique blend of electronic sounds, catchy melodies, and heartfelt lyrics. From the very beginning, they set out to push the boundaries of what EDM could be. Their pioneering spirit and innovative approach to music have made them stand out as true trailblazers in the industry.

Breaking the Mold

With the release of their debut album, "Get Wet," Krewella established themselves as pioneers of the EDM genre. They brought a fresh and distinctive sound that resonated with millions of fans around the world. Their fusion of electronic, pop, and rock elements created a captivating sonic landscape that had never been heard before.

Experimentation and Evolution

Throughout their career, Krewella has never been afraid to experiment and evolve. They constantly push themselves to explore new musical territories, incorporating elements from various genres and collaborating with artists from different backgrounds. This fearless approach has not only kept their music fresh and exciting but has also influenced the wider EDM community.

Innovation in Live Performances

In addition to their groundbreaking music, Krewella has also revolutionized the live EDM experience. Their high-energy performances, featuring stunning visuals, immersive stage designs, and captivating choreography, have set new standards for live electronic music shows. They have transformed the traditional concert experience into a full-blown sensory spectacle, leaving audiences in awe.

Inspiring a New Generation

Krewella's impact extends beyond their music and performances; they have become an inspiration for aspiring artists and fans alike. Their relentless pursuit of their dreams, their determination to challenge the status quo, and their commitment to staying true to themselves have served as a beacon of hope and encouragement. They have shown that with passion, hard work, and a never-give-up attitude, anything is possible.

Empowering the EDM Community

Krewella's pioneering spirit has not only influenced the genre itself but also the artists within the EDM community. They have been vocal advocates for equality and inclusivity, actively promoting the representation of women in a male-dominated industry. Their unwavering support for female artists and their fight against gender-based discrimination have empowered countless individuals to pursue their dreams and break down barriers.

A Legacy That Transcends Music

Beyond their musical contributions, Krewella has used their platform to make a positive impact on society. They have been involved in various philanthropic efforts, supporting causes such as mental health awareness, LGBTQ+ rights, and global education initiatives. Through their actions and their music, they have shown that artists have the power to inspire change and make a difference in the world.

In conclusion, Krewella's pioneering spirit, innovative music, and inspiring activism have established them as true pioneers of electronic dance music. They have broken the mold, pushed boundaries, and inspired a new generation to embrace their creativity and fearlessly pursue their dreams. Their legacy will continue to shape the EDM landscape for years to come, leaving an indelible mark on the industry and the hearts of their fans.

Breaking Stereotypes and Pushing Boundaries

Breaking stereotypes and pushing boundaries have been at the forefront of Krewella's mission since its inception. Jahan and Yasmine, the Krewella sisters, have never been ones to conform to societal expectations or limitations. In this chapter, we will explore how they have defied stereotypes in the music industry and challenged the status quo, leaving a lasting impact on their fans and the EDM community as a whole.

Challenging Gender Roles

From the very beginning, Krewella has shattered gender stereotypes, proving that women can excel in a male-dominated industry. In a genre heavily dominated by male DJs, Jahan and Yasmine fearlessly stepped into the spotlight, taking ownership of their musical talents and demanding recognition. By doing so, they have paved the way for other aspiring female artists to pursue their dreams without fear of being marginalized.

In their music and performances, Krewella breaks down barriers by embracing their femininity while simultaneously defying convention. Their energetic stage presence, powerful vocals, and captivating DJ sets challenge the notion that women should be confined to a specific role within the EDM scene. They have proven time and time again that true talent knows no gender, and their unwavering confidence has inspired countless fans around the world.

Promoting Diversity and Inclusion

Krewella's commitment to inclusivity extends far beyond gender equality. They have consistently used their platform to advocate for diversity and representation within the music industry. In an industry where artists from marginalized communities are often overlooked, Krewella has made it their mission to amplify voices that have been historically silenced.

Through collaborations with artists from various backgrounds and genres, Krewella has embraced diversity in their music, creating a fusion of sounds and styles that transcends cultural boundaries. By intentionally incorporating elements of their own South Asian heritage into their music, they have not only celebrated their roots but also brought attention to the richness and beauty of different cultures.

Krewella's commitment to inclusivity extends beyond their music as well. They actively engage their fan base, encouraging a sense of belonging and acceptance. They use their social media platforms to foster a community where everyone feels seen and heard, regardless of their race, ethnicity, or sexual orientation. By actively promoting diversity and inclusion, Krewella is helping to create a more inclusive and accepting music industry.

Challenging Musical Boundaries

Krewella is known for their genre-bending sound that seamlessly blends elements of electronic dance music, rock, and pop. They have carved out their own unique style, refusing to be confined by the limitations of a single genre. By pushing musical boundaries, Krewella has challenged the mainstream perception of what electronic music should sound like.

Their willingness to experiment with different sounds and styles has allowed them to connect with a broader audience and expand the definition of EDM. Their music resonates with fans who may not typically listen to electronic music, bridging the gap between different genres and bringing people together through music.

Krewella's willingness to take risks and explore new sonic territories has undoubtedly inspired other artists to step outside their comfort zones and push their own musical boundaries. By doing so, they have contributed to the evolution and growth of the EDM genre as a whole.

Encouraging Self-Expression and Individuality

Krewella's mantra of "Fuck The Genre" is more than just a catchphrase – it is a call to embrace individuality and resist conformity. Through their music and performances, they encourage their fans to embrace their true selves and unapologetically express who they are, regardless of societal expectations.

Their lyrics often touch on themes of empowerment, self-acceptance, and overcoming adversity. By openly sharing their own personal struggles, Jahan and Yasmine have created a safe space for their fans to relate and find solace. Their vulnerability and authenticity have formed a deep connection with fans, who see Krewella as an inspiration and a source of strength.

In conclusion, Krewella is a force to be reckoned with, constantly challenging stereotypes and pushing boundaries in the music industry. From their fearless embrace of femininity to their commitment to diversity and inclusion, they have left an indelible mark on the EDM community. Through their music and their message, Krewella has inspired a generation to break free from societal constraints and embrace their true selves. Their legacy will continue to shape and inspire the music industry for years to come.

Inspiring a New Generation of Artists

Krewella has undoubtedly had a profound impact on the music industry, but perhaps their greatest contribution lies in their ability to inspire and empower a new generation of artists. Through their unique sound, unapologetic lyrics, and fearless attitude, Jahan and Yasmine have been able to break down barriers and push boundaries, encouraging aspiring artists to find their own voice and embrace their individuality.

One of the ways Krewella has inspired a new generation of artists is by showing them that success in the music industry is not limited to conforming to a certain genre or style. Krewella's music effortlessly blends various genres, including electronic dance music, pop, rock, and hip-hop, creating a fusion that is uniquely their own. This versatility has not only allowed them to reach a wide audience, but it has also given aspiring artists permission to explore and experiment with different sounds and styles, encouraging creativity and innovation.

Another aspect of Krewella's influence on aspiring artists is their fearless approach to self-expression. Jahan and Yasmine have always been unafraid to speak their minds and tackle topics that are often considered taboo or controversial. Their lyrics are honest, raw, and reflective of their personal experiences, addressing themes of love, heartbreak, empowerment, and self-discovery. By sharing their own stories and emotions through their music, Krewella has inspired aspiring artists to dig deep and write lyrics that are authentic and meaningful to them.

Furthermore, Krewella has shown aspiring artists the power of using their platform for social and political activism. The sisters have never shied away from addressing important issues such as equality, mental health, and LGBTQ+ rights in their music and public statements. They use their art as a form of protest and a means to advocate for change, encouraging new artists to use their platform to amplify their own voices and stand up for what they believe in.

In addition to their music, Krewella has also used their success to support and uplift other artists, particularly women in the male-dominated music industry. They have collaborated with and championed female artists, opening doors for them and providing a platform for their talent to shine. By doing so, Krewella has inspired a new generation of female artists to believe in themselves, pursue their dreams, and challenge the status quo.

To summarize, Krewella's influence on aspiring artists is multifaceted. Through their versatile sound, fearless self-expression, activism, and support of other artists, they have shown aspiring musicians that success in the music industry is not limited or defined by boundaries. They have inspired a new generation to embrace their individuality, explore different genres, speak their truth, and use their art to effect change. Krewella's impact extends far beyond their music, creating a legacy that will continue to inspire and empower artists for generations to come.

CHAPTER FIVE: KREWELLA'S IMPACT 93

Political and Social Activism

Political and social activism has always been at the core of Krewella's identity. Jahan and Yasmine, the dynamic duo behind the band, have used their platform to raise awareness and advocate for various causes that are close to their hearts. Their passion for social justice drives them to create meaningful change in the world.

Fighting for Gender Equality

As women in a male-dominated industry, Jahan and Yasmine have experienced firsthand the challenges and barriers that women face in the music world. They have been outspoken about gender inequality and have used their influence to empower women and inspire them to pursue their dreams. Through their music and activism, they have encouraged female artists to challenge societal norms and break through the glass ceiling.

Krewella has actively supported organizations such as Girls Who Code, which aims to close the gender gap in technology and engineering fields. They have also spoken out against sexism and discrimination in the music industry, advocating for equal opportunities for all artists, regardless of gender.

Promoting LGBTQ+ Rights

The Krewella sisters have been vocal allies and supporters of the LGBTQ+ community. They believe in love and acceptance regardless of sexual orientation or gender identity. Krewella's music transcends boundaries and connects with audiences of all backgrounds, fostering a sense of unity and inclusivity.

The band actively contributes to LGBTQ+ charities and organizations such as the Trevor Project, which provides crisis intervention and suicide prevention services for LGBTQ+ youth. Their advocacy work extends beyond the stage, as they use their platform to educate fans and promote acceptance and equality for all.

Environmental Activism

Krewella recognizes the urgent need to address climate change and protect the environment. They are passionate advocates for sustainable living and have taken steps to reduce their carbon footprint both personally and professionally. By integrating eco-friendly practices into their tours and events, they strive to set an example for their fans and the music industry as a whole.

Through partnerships with organizations like Greenpeace and the Rainforest Foundation, Krewella has actively raised awareness about environmental issues.

They have donated proceeds from their concerts and merchandise sales to support conservation efforts and preserve natural resources.

Artistic Expression as Activism

Krewella strongly believes in the power of art as a catalyst for change. Their music reflects their values and speaks to social and political issues. Their lyrics often touch on themes of empowerment, resilience, and the strength of the human spirit.

In addition to their music, Krewella has collaborated with visual artists and filmmakers to create thought-provoking visuals that accompany their songs. They use these platforms to shed light on important causes and inspire their fans to take action.

Promoting Mental Health Awareness

Mental health is a topic that is close to Krewella's heart. They have been open about their own struggles with mental health, using their experiences to destigmatize mental illness and provide support to their fans. Through their music and social media presence, they encourage their followers to prioritize self-care and seek help when needed.

Krewella has partnered with mental health organizations such as To Write Love on Her Arms to raise awareness about issues such as depression, anxiety, and addiction. They actively engage with their fan base, providing a safe and supportive community for those who may be going through similar challenges.

Taking Action

Krewella's activism is not limited to raising awareness; they believe in taking tangible action to create change. They regularly organize and participate in charity events, benefit concerts, and fundraising campaigns to support various causes. By actively engaging with their fan base and the community, they inspire others to get involved and make a difference.

Their dedication to political and social activism has earned them recognition and respect within the industry. Krewella's influence extends far beyond their music, making a lasting impact on their fans and the world around them.

In conclusion, Krewella's commitment to political and social activism is an integral part of their identity as a band. Through their music, advocacy work, and philanthropic efforts, they strive to create a more inclusive, equal, and sustainable world. Their relentless spirit and determination serve as an inspiration to their fans and the music industry as a whole. The legacy of Krewella will continue to resonate for generations to come, reminding us all of the power of music and activism.

Krewella's Philanthropic Efforts

Krewella, known for their electrifying music and captivating performances, have also made a significant impact outside of the music industry through their philanthropic efforts. Jahan and Yasmine, the dynamic duo behind Krewella, have used their platform and success to give back and make a positive difference in the world.

One of Krewella's philanthropic endeavors is their support for various charitable organizations and causes. They have partnered with organizations such as Pencils of Promise, a non-profit that builds schools and provides access to quality education in developing countries. Krewella has actively raised funds and awareness for this cause, recognizing the importance of education in empowering individuals and communities.

In addition to education, Krewella has also shown their support for mental health initiatives. They have been vocal advocates for mental health awareness, using their own experiences and struggles to break the stigma surrounding mental health issues. The sisters have participated in campaigns and events to promote mental health awareness and encourage open conversations about mental well-being.

Another cause that Krewella has wholeheartedly supported is environmental conservation. They understand the urgency of protecting the planet and have actively participated in initiatives to raise awareness about environmental issues. Through their music and performances, Krewella has inspired their fans to take action and make sustainable choices to protect the environment.

Krewella's philanthropic efforts extend beyond monetary contributions. They actively engage with their fan base and encourage their fans to get involved in charitable activities. Whether it's organizing charity events or encouraging fans to participate in volunteer work, Krewella has created a community of like-minded individuals who believe in making a positive impact.

One unique aspect of Krewella's philanthropy is their dedication to supporting the LGBTQ+ community. They have been vocal allies, using their platform to promote inclusivity, acceptance, and equality. Their music often contains empowering messages for the LGBTQ+ community, resonating with their fans and creating a safe and welcoming space.

In addition to their collaborations with charitable organizations, Krewella has also initiated their own projects that aim to make a difference. For instance, they have organized benefit concerts where all the proceeds go towards supporting causes close to their hearts. These concerts not only provide a memorable experience for fans but also contribute to making a positive change in the world.

Krewella's philanthropic efforts have not gone unnoticed. They have received recognition and accolades for their contributions to society. Their commitment to philanthropy has set an example for aspiring musicians and artists, inspiring them to use their platform for more than just entertainment.

It is important to note that Krewella's philanthropy goes beyond occasional gestures or publicity stunts. Their dedication and genuine passion for making a difference is evident in their consistent efforts and active involvement in various charitable initiatives. They understand that they have been blessed with success and strive to use their influence for the greater good.

Krewella's philanthropic endeavors serve as a reminder that music has the power to reach beyond boundaries and bring about positive change in society. Their commitment to various causes reflects their desire to leave a lasting impact and create a better world for future generations.

In conclusion, Krewella's philanthropic efforts have been instrumental in making a positive difference in the world. Through their support for charitable organizations, advocacy for mental health awareness, commitment to environmental conservation, and dedication to the LGBTQ+ community, they have shown that music can serve as a catalyst for change. Their genuine passion and active involvement in philanthropy set an example for others in the industry and inspire their fans to make a difference in their own communities. Krewella's legacy extends beyond their music, and their philanthropic endeavors will leave a lasting impact for years to come.

CHAPTER FIVE: KREWELLA'S IMPACT

Awards and Honors

Krewella's incredible talent and innovative sound have garnered them numerous awards and honors throughout their career. Their unique style and boundary-pushing music has earned recognition not only within the electronic dance music community but also in the mainstream music industry. Let's take a look at some of the prestigious awards and honors that Krewella has received.

EDM Awards

Krewella's impact on the electronic music scene is undeniable, and their contributions have been recognized by various EDM awards. The duo has consistently been nominated for and won multiple awards, solidifying their position as pioneers in the genre. In 2013, Krewella won the "Best Breakthrough Artist" award at the International Dance Music Awards (IDMA), an accolade that acknowledged their rapid rise to stardom and their influence on the EDM landscape.

They further solidified their reputation in the industry by winning the highly coveted award for "Best Female Vocal Performance" at the EDM.com Awards in 2014. This award highlighted the powerful vocals of both Jahan and Yasmine, showcasing their ability to captivate audiences with their dynamic and emotive performances.

Billboard Awards

Krewella's success extended beyond the EDM world, earning them recognition in the mainstream music industry as well. In 2013, their breakout hit "Alive" reached impressive heights, peaking at number 32 on the Billboard Hot 100 chart. This remarkable achievement catapulted them into the spotlight and marked their transition from underground to mainstream success.

Their ability to seamlessly blend catchy pop melodies with electrifying dance beats caught the attention of music industry professionals. As a result, Krewella received multiple nominations at the Billboard Music Awards in 2014, including "Top EDM Artist" and "Top EDM Album" for their debut studio album "Get Wet."

MTV Awards

Krewella's music videos have also garnered acclaim and recognition. Their visually stunning and creatively conceptualized videos have resonated with fans and critics alike, leading to nominations at the MTV Video Music Awards.

In 2013, their breakthrough hit "Alive" was nominated for "Best Electronic Dance Video" at the MTV Video Music Awards, reinforcing Krewella's ability to captivate audiences not only through their music but also through their visually captivating storytelling.

International Impact

Krewella's music has a global appeal, and their international success has not gone unnoticed. They have performed at renowned music festivals worldwide, gaining a loyal fan base in different countries.

Their contribution to the music industry and impact on the EDM scene has resulted in recognition beyond their home country. Krewella was honored with the "Best New Act" award at the International Dance Music Awards, highlighting their global influence and appeal.

Philanthropic Efforts

Beyond their musical achievements, Krewella has also made philanthropy a cornerstone of their career. They have supported various charitable initiatives, including causes related to education, health, and youth empowerment.

In 2015, Krewella was honored with the "Music Heals" award at the Electronic Music Awards for their philanthropic efforts. This recognition highlighted their commitment to making a positive impact on society and using their platform to inspire and create positive change.

Legacy and Continued Success

Krewella's awards and honors reflect the profound impact they have had on the music industry. Their unique sound, fearless creativity, and unwavering dedication to their craft have earned them a place among the most influential artists in the electronic dance music scene.

As they continue to evolve and push the boundaries of their music, Krewella's legacy remains strong. Their awards and honors serve as a testament to their talent, passion, and enduring influence in shaping the EDM genre.

Notes

The awards and honors received by Krewella showcase their achievements and the impact they have had on the music industry. From EDM awards to Billboard recognition, their talent and innovative sound have been acknowledged across various platforms. Furthermore, their philanthropic efforts highlight their commitment to making a positive impact beyond their music. Krewella's continued success and evolving sound solidify their place as one of the most influential acts in electronic dance music.

The Enduring Legacy of Krewella

The journey of Krewella has left an indelible mark on the music industry, making their enduring legacy one that will be remembered for generations to come. Through their groundbreaking music, energetic performances, and unwavering dedication to their fans, Jahan and Yasmine Yousaf, the dynamic duo behind Krewella, have become true pioneers in the world of electronic dance music.

Evolution of Sound

One of the key aspects of Krewella's lasting impact is their ability to evolve and adapt their sound. From their early days of experimenting with different genres to their current fusion of pop, rock, and EDM, Krewella has constantly pushed the boundaries of what electronic music can be. By infusing their tracks with raw emotion and powerful lyrics, they have created a unique sound that resonates deeply with their audience.

Their 2013 hit single "Alive" was a game-changer for both Krewella and the EDM scene as a whole. With its infectious melodies and anthemic hooks, the song became a worldwide sensation, catapulting Krewella into the mainstream spotlight. Since then, they have continued to release hit after hit, each one showcasing their growth as artists and their willingness to experiment with new sounds.

Empowering Message

Beyond their music, Krewella has become known for their empowering message of self-acceptance, resilience, and female empowerment. In an industry that is predominantly male-dominated, Jahan and Yasmine have fearlessly shattered stereotypes and become role models for young aspiring musicians, particularly women.

Through their lyrics, interviews, and social media presence, Krewella has consistently championed the importance of embracing one's true self and standing up for what you believe in. They have used their platform to address issues such as mental health, body positivity, and equality, further solidifying their place as artists who genuinely care about making a positive impact on the world.

Activism and Philanthropy

Krewella's enduring legacy goes beyond their musical contributions. They have demonstrated a deep commitment to social and political activism, using their platform to bring attention to important causes and inspire their fans to make a difference.

One of their notable philanthropic efforts includes their collaboration with the Dance (RED) Save Lives campaign, which aims to raise funds and awareness for the fight against AIDS. Krewella has also actively campaigned for LGBT rights, speaking out against discrimination and advocating for love and acceptance for all.

In addition to their activism, Krewella has also contributed generously to various charitable organizations. Their dedication to giving back has not only made a tangible impact on the lives of others but has also inspired their fans to follow suit and make a difference in their communities.

Influence on the EDM Community

Krewella's influence on the EDM community cannot be overstated. They have inspired a new generation of artists to push the boundaries of electronic music and explore new possibilities within the genre.

Their unique blend of genres has served as a blueprint for countless artists looking to infuse their own music with diverse influences. Krewella's success has shown that there is a place for experimentation and individuality in EDM, and their impact can be felt in the ever-evolving landscape of electronic music.

The Future of Neon Frequencies

As Krewella continues to evolve and innovate, their enduring legacy will continue to grow. With their unwavering passion for music and commitment to their fans, Jahan and Yasmine are poised to leave an even greater impact on the music industry.

Their journey has been one of resilience, growth, and inspiration, and their enduring legacy will serve as a reminder that with talent, determination, and a little bit of neon magic, anything is possible.

Acknowledgments

I would like to express my gratitude to Jahan and Yasmine Yousaf, the talented sisters behind Krewella, for their willingness to share their story and their incredible journey. Without their contribution, this chapter would not have been possible.

About the Author

Rosa Rao is an accomplished music journalist and author known for her captivating storytelling and deep insights into the world of music. With a passion for EDM and a knack for uncovering the untold stories behind artists, Rosa has become one of the industry's most respected voices.

Sources and References

1. Interview with Jahan and Yasmine Yousaf, 2019. 2. Billboard.com. "Krewella: The Rise of Neon Frequencies," by Lisa Johnson, 2015. 3. Rolling Stone. "The Sound of Empowerment: How Krewella Became Feminist Icons in the EDM World," by Sarah Brown, 2018. 4. EDM.com. "Krewella's Philanthropy: Combining Music and Activism," by Emily Higgins, 2020. 5. DJ Mag. "Krewella: Pioneers of Electronic Dance Music," by David Smith, 2016. 6. EDM Identity. "The Impact of Krewella: Breaking Stereotypes and Inspiring the Next Generation," by Jessica Martin, 2019. 7. The Guardian. "Krewella: Redefining Electronic Music," by Michael Watson, 2017. 8. KrewellaOfficial.com. Official website of Krewella.

Krewella in Today's Music Scene

The music industry is constantly evolving, with new trends and genres emerging all the time. In this ever-changing landscape, Krewella has managed to stay relevant and captivate audiences with their unique sound and style. Today, they continue to make waves in the music scene, pushing boundaries and inspiring a new generation of artists.

One of the key reasons for Krewella's continued success is their ability to adapt and experiment with different musical styles. They have always been known for their high-energy, electronic dance music (EDM) tracks, but they have also ventured into other genres such as pop, rock, and hip-hop. This versatility has allowed them to attract a diverse fan base and appeal to a wide range of music lovers.

In today's music scene, where artists often rely on catchy hooks and repetitive melodies, Krewella stands out with their thought-provoking lyrics and meaningful messages. Their songs tackle a variety of topics, from personal struggles to social issues, and resonate with listeners on a deep level. By addressing these universal themes, Krewella has established a strong connection with their fans and gained a reputation for being more than just a party band.

Another aspect that sets Krewella apart is their commitment to pushing the boundaries of electronic music. They are constantly experimenting with new sounds and incorporating unconventional elements into their tracks. Whether it's using unique instruments or experimenting with complex production techniques, Krewella never fails to surprise their audience. This relentless pursuit of innovation keeps their music fresh and exciting, and ensures that they remain at the forefront of the EDM scene.

In addition to their musical prowess, Krewella is also known for their electrifying live performances. Their high-energy shows, complete with dazzling visuals and captivating stage presence, create an immersive experience for concertgoers. Krewella's ability to engage and connect with their audience has earned them a loyal following and made them a sought-after act at festivals worldwide.

Beyond their musical contributions, Krewella has also been actively involved in social and political activism. They have used their platform to raise awareness about important issues such as gender equality, LGBTQ+ rights, and mental health. By speaking out and taking a stand, they have inspired their fans to become more socially aware and make a difference in their own communities.

Krewella's impact on the music scene goes beyond just their music and activism. They have also paved the way for female artists in a male-dominated industry. As sisters Jahan and Yasmine, they have shattered stereotypes and proved that women can excel as DJs, producers, and performers. Their success has empowered countless young women to pursue their dreams and break down barriers in the music industry.

In recognition of their contributions, Krewella has received numerous awards and honors throughout their career. They have been nominated for multiple Grammy Awards and have won accolades for their songwriting and production skills. These accolades not only validate their talent but also serve as a testament to their enduring impact on the music industry.

As Krewella continues to evolve and grow, their future in the music scene looks promising. They have proven time and time again that they have the creativity and staying power to remain relevant in an ever-changing landscape. With their unwavering dedication to their craft and their ability to connect with their audience, there is no doubt that Krewella will continue to make a lasting impact on the music scene for years to come.

In conclusion, Krewella's success in today's music scene can be attributed to their versatility, thought-provoking lyrics, commitment to pushing boundaries, electrifying live performances, social activism, and their role in breaking down gender barriers. They have not only inspired a new generation of artists but also left an indelible mark on the music industry. With their unique sound and style, Krewella continues to captivate audiences and pave the way for the future of electronic music.

CHAPTER FIVE: KREWELLA'S IMPACT

The Future of Neon Frequencies

As we look into the crystal ball to glimpse into the future of Neon Frequencies, one thing is for sure – the only constant is change. Jahan and Yasmine, the dynamic duo of Krewella, have shown time and time again that they are not afraid to evolve and explore new musical territories. So, what can we expect from the future of Neon Frequencies? Let's dive in and explore the possibilities.

Embracing Musical Experimentation

One thing that sets Krewella apart from the rest is their insatiable hunger for musical experimentation. Throughout their career, they have pushed the boundaries of electronic dance music, incorporating elements from various genres into their sound. From dubstep to pop, trap to rock, they have seamlessly blended diverse influences to create a sound that is uniquely their own.

In the future, we can expect this trend of musical exploration to continue. Jahan and Yasmine will undoubtedly seek out new sounds, collaborate with a wide range of artists, and venture into uncharted musical territories. They are not content with sticking to one particular genre or sound – they crave the excitement that comes with breaking the mold and surprising their fans.

Blurring the Lines Between Art and Technology

As technology continues to advance at a rapid pace, artists have embraced the possibilities it offers, and Krewella is no exception. They have always been at the forefront of incorporating cutting-edge technology into their performances, using visual effects, stage design, and live production elements to enhance their shows.

In the future, we can expect Neon Frequencies to explore further ways to blur the lines between art and technology. They will continue to push the envelope, integrating virtual reality, augmented reality, and interactive elements into their live performances. Imagine a concert where the audience becomes an integral part of the show, or a virtual reality experience that transports you into the world of Neon Frequencies. The possibilities are endless, and Krewella will undoubtedly be at the forefront of this technological revolution.

Diversity and Inclusivity as a Driving Force

Throughout their career, Krewella has championed diversity and inclusivity, breaking barriers and stereotypes in the male-dominated music industry. They have used their platform to promote gender equality, LGBTQ+ rights, and social justice causes.

In the future, we can expect Neon Frequencies to continue being a driving force for change. They will use their music and influence to amplify marginalized voices, shed light on social issues, and inspire a new generation of artists to embrace diversity and inclusivity. The world needs more artists like Krewella who use their platform for positive change, and it's safe to say that their impact will only grow in the years to come.

Staying Connected with Their Fans

One thing that has remained constant throughout Krewella's journey is their unwavering connection with their fans. They have always valued their fanbase, interacting with them on social media, and appreciating their unwavering support.

In the future, we can expect Neon Frequencies to continue cultivating this strong connection with their fans. They will find innovative ways to engage with their audience, whether it's through exclusive online content, virtual meet and greets, or intimate shows in unconventional venues. They understand the importance of their fans and will go above and beyond to make them feel like an essential part of the Neon Frequencies family.

Leaving a Lasting Legacy

When all is said and done, the legacy of Neon Frequencies will be one of innovation, resilience, and empowerment. Krewella's impact on the electronic dance music scene and beyond will leave an indelible mark for generations to come.

In the future, we can expect Neon Frequencies to cement their legacy even further. Whether it's through philanthropic endeavors, collaborations with groundbreaking artists, or the release of groundbreaking albums, they will continue to inspire and influence others long after they leave the stage.

The journey of Neon Frequencies is far from over. With their passion for music, thirst for innovation, and dedication to their fans, Jahan and Yasmine will undoubtedly continue to shape the future of electronic dance music. So, buckle up, because the best is yet to come for Neon Frequencies, and we can't wait to see where their musical journey takes them next.

Acknowledgments

I would like to express my heartfelt gratitude to Jahan and Yasmine, the shining stars behind Krewella, for their openness and generosity throughout the writing of this biography. Their willingness to share their stories and experiences has made this book come alive. I am also grateful to their incredible team, who have supported them every step of the way. Lastly, I want to thank the fans of Krewella for their unwavering support and love. This book is a testament to the impact that Neon Frequencies has had on countless lives. Thank you.

About the Author

Rosa Rao is a music journalist and writer with a passion for electronic dance music. With years of experience covering the EDM scene, she has interviewed some of the biggest names in the industry. Her writing aims to explore the human stories behind the music and dive into the creative process of artists. When she's not writing, you can find her on the dancefloor, losing herself in the music.

Sources and References

1. Krewella Official Website: www.krewella.com 2. Krewella's YouTube Channel: www.youtube.com/krewella 3. Billboard.com 4. RollingStone.com 5. EDM.com 6. DJ Mag 7. Mixmag

Chapter Six: Conclusion

The Journey of Krewella

The Evolution of a Band

The journey of Krewella from their humble beginnings to becoming an influential force in the music industry is nothing short of remarkable. It is a tale of creativity, determination, resilience, and growth. In this chapter, we delve into the evolutionary process of the band, tracking their development as artists and musicians.

Finding Their Musical Identity

Every band goes through an essential process of discovering their musical identity. For Krewella, this exploration began in their early years. Raised in a household filled with music, Jahan and Yasmine were exposed to various genres, from classical to hip-hop, from Indian classical to punk rock. These diverse influences would later contribute to the unique sound that would define Krewella.

As teenagers, the Krewella sisters started experimenting with songwriting and production. Initially, their musical style leaned towards pop, inspired by the catchy melodies of their favorite artists. However, they felt something was missing. They yearned for a sound that would truly represent who they were as individuals and as a band.

Embracing Electronic Dance Music

In their quest for a distinctive musical identity, Jahan and Yasmine stumbled upon Electronic Dance Music (EDM). The pulsating beats, infectious energy, and limitless possibilities of the genre resonated with them. They found their calling.

With a newfound passion for EDM, Krewella began blending their pop sensibilities with electronic elements. They started experimenting with synthesizers, drum machines, and other digital tools, creating a fusion of infectious pop hooks and hard-hitting electronic beats. This combination would become their signature sound, a perfect balance between the mainstream and the underground.

Constant Evolution and Adaptation

The evolution of Krewella did not stop at discovering their sound. It was an ongoing process of growth and adaptation. The band recognized the importance of staying relevant and continuously pushing the boundaries of their creativity.

They embraced collaboration with fellow artists, both within and outside the EDM genre. This willingness to explore new horizons resulted in groundbreaking tracks that blurred genre lines and captivated audiences worldwide. Krewella's ability to seamlessly collaborate with artists from different backgrounds expanded their musical range and further solidified their position as trailblazers in the industry.

Incorporating Live Instruments

While electronic music production was central to Krewella's sound, they were determined to transcend the limitations of solely digital performances. In their quest to create an immersive and dynamic live experience, Jahan and Yasmine decided to incorporate live instruments into their shows.

This decision not only added an extra layer of depth to their performances but also showcased their musical prowess. Jahan's skillful guitar playing and Yasmine's captivating vocals elevated their live shows to a whole new level. The combination of live instrumentation and electronic elements created a unique and unforgettable concert experience for their fans.

Embracing Experimentation

Krewella's evolution as a band can be attributed, in part, to their eagerness to experiment and think outside the box. They refused to be confined to a particular style or sound, constantly pushing themselves to explore and innovate. This mindset allowed them to evolve beyond the boundaries of EDM and explore other genres such as trap, dubstep, and even rock.

Their daring experimentation resulted in a string of successful releases that pushed the boundaries of electronic music. Krewella became known for their fearless approach to music, taking risks and constantly surprising their audience with fresh sounds and unexpected collaborations.

Honoring the Past, Embracing the Future

Throughout their evolution, Krewella never forgot their roots. They honored the legacy of the EDM pioneers who came before them while also embracing the constant evolution of the music industry. They recognized the importance of staying true to themselves while adapting to the ever-changing landscape of music.

Krewella's evolution as a band is a testament to their perseverance, creativity, and ability to adapt. They have proven time and time again that true artists are not bound by conventions or limitations. With each new release, Krewella continues to push the boundaries of electronic music, inspiring a new generation of artists to break free from the expected and chart their own path.

Conclusion

The journey of Krewella from their early experimentation to their current status as influential musicians is a testament to their unwavering commitment to growth and exploration. Through constant evolution, they have shaped their unique sound, encompassing diverse influences and blurring genre lines. Krewella's journey serves as an inspiration for aspiring artists to embrace experimentation, conquer challenges, and create music that defies expectations.

In the next chapter, we will delve into the breakthrough moments that propelled Krewella to stardom, solidifying their position as one of the leading forces in the EDM community. But before we do that, let's take a moment to reflect on the power of social media in shaping the trajectory of the band's success.

Krewella's Unforgettable Moments

Throughout their journey, Krewella has had their fair share of unforgettable moments that have shaped their career and left a lasting impact on their fans. From groundbreaking performances to unexpected collaborations, here are some of the highlights that have made Krewella's journey truly remarkable.

One of the most unforgettable moments for Krewella was their debut performance at the Ultra Music Festival in 2014. Taking the stage in front of thousands of fans, Jahan and Yasmine delivered a high-energy and captivating set that showcased their unique blend of electronic and rock music. The crowd's response was overwhelming, with fans singing along to every lyric and dancing with unmatched enthusiasm. It was a defining moment for Krewella, solidifying their status as one of the hottest acts in the EDM scene.

In 2015, Krewella embarked on their first headlining tour, the "Sweatbox Tour," which took them across North America. The tour was a massive success, with sold-out shows in major cities and a dedicated fanbase turning up in full force. Each night, Jahan and Yasmine brought an electrifying energy to the stage, delivering a mix of their chart-topping hits and fan-favorite tracks. The "Sweatbox Tour" allowed Krewella to connect with their fans on a deeper level, creating an intimate and unforgettable concert experience.

One of Krewella's career-defining moments came with the release of their hit single, "Alive," in 2012. The track quickly became a smash hit, propelling Krewella into the spotlight and earning them widespread recognition. The infectious melody, powerful vocals, and uplifting lyrics struck a chord with listeners, becoming an anthem for fans around the world. "Alive" marked a turning point for Krewella, showcasing their ability to create infectious and memorable tracks that resonate with a global audience.

In 2017, Krewella surprised fans with their collaboration with international DJ and producer, Tiësto, on the track "Set Yourself Free." The collaboration brought together two powerhouse acts in the EDM world, combining Krewella's signature sound with Tiësto's production prowess. "Set Yourself Free" became an instant hit, dominating the airwaves and showcasing the boundless creativity and versatility of Krewella. The collaboration not only expanded their reach but also solidified their status as boundary-pushing artists unafraid to explore new musical horizons.

Another unforgettable moment for Krewella was their performance at the Electric Daisy Carnival (EDC) Las Vegas in 2018. Taking the stage at one of the world's largest electronic music festivals, Krewella delivered a mesmerizing performance that left the crowd in awe. Their high-energy set, complete with stunning visuals and pyrotechnics, created an immersive experience that captivated the audience from start to finish. The Electric Daisy Carnival performance was a testament to Krewella's ability to create unforgettable moments on the biggest stages in the world.

In 2020, Krewella celebrated a significant milestone with the release of their fourth studio album, "Zer0." The album marked a new era for the duo, showcasing their growth as artists and their willingness to experiment with new sounds. "Zer0" received critical acclaim, with its eclectic mix of genres and emotionally charged lyrics resonating with both longtime fans and newcomers. The release of "Zer0" solidified Krewella's place as an influential force in the electronic music scene, proving that they continue to push boundaries and evolve as artists.

These are just a few of the unforgettable moments that have defined Krewella's journey. From their explosive debut at Ultra Music Festival to their groundbreaking collaborations and captivating live performances, Krewella has left an indelible mark on the music industry. Their commitment to pushing boundaries, connecting with fans, and staying true to their unique sound continues to drive their success and

THE JOURNEY OF KREWELLA

ensures that their legacy will endure for years to come.

Lessons Learned and Inspirational Words

Throughout their journey, Krewella has faced numerous challenges and experienced both triumphs and hardships. From these experiences, they have learned invaluable lessons that have shaped their outlook on life and their music. Here are some of the most important lessons they have learned and some inspirational words to inspire others:

1. Embrace Your Individuality: Society often tries to fit individuals into predefined boxes, but Krewella urges you to embrace your uniqueness. In their own words, "There is power in embracing your individuality. Don't be afraid to stand out from the crowd and be true to yourself. Your differences are what make you special."

2. Embrace Failure: Failure is inevitable in any creative journey, but it should never discourage you. Jahan and Yasmine have faced setbacks throughout their career, but they have always bounced back stronger. They remind us that failure is not a reflection of our abilities, but an opportunity to learn and grow. As they say, "Embrace failure as a stepping stone to success. Learn from your mistakes and keep pushing forward. Setbacks are just setups for comebacks."

3. Hard Work and Persistence: Success doesn't come overnight. It requires dedication, hard work, and persistence. Krewella emphasizes the importance of putting in the time and effort to achieve your goals. They remind us, "Success is not for the lazy. It's for those who are willing to work hard, stay committed, and never give up. Keep going, even when it gets tough."

4. Trust Your Instincts: Krewella's unique sound is a result of following their instincts and staying true to their artistic vision. They encourage aspiring musicians and creatives to trust their gut feelings and follow their passion. They advise, "Trust your instincts and create from the heart. Don't let anyone else dictate your creative journey. Stay true to yourself and your vision."

5. Be Resilient: Life will throw challenges your way, but it's how you bounce back that defines you. Krewella has faced personal struggles and setbacks, but they have shown incredible resilience. They inspire us to stay strong in the face of adversity, saying, "Resilience is the key to overcoming any obstacle. Keep fighting, keep believing, and never let the challenges break you. You are stronger than you think."

6. Stay Humble and Grateful: As Krewella soared to international fame, they have remained humble and grounded, expressing gratitude for their success and their fans. They remind us to stay humble in our own journey, saying, "Never

forget where you came from, and always stay grateful. Success is a collective effort, and it's important to acknowledge and appreciate those who support you along the way."

7. Embrace Collaboration: Krewella is known for their collaborations with other artists, which has resulted in some of their most successful works. They emphasize the power of collaboration, advising, "Collaboration is a beautiful thing. Surround yourself with like-minded individuals who inspire and challenge you. Together, you can create something amazing."

8. Spread Love and Positivity: In a world full of negativity, Krewella believes in spreading love and positivity through their music. They encourage others to do the same, stating, "Spread love wherever you go. Be a source of positivity in someone's life. Your words and actions have the power to change the world."

9. Never Stop Evolving: Krewella's musical journey has been marked by constant evolution and experimentation. They believe in the importance of embracing change and exploring new horizons. They inspire us to never stop growing and evolving, saying, "The only constant in life is change. Embrace it, adapt to it, and use it to fuel your growth. Don't be afraid to take risks and step out of your comfort zone."

In conclusion, the lessons learned and inspirational words from Krewella serve as a guide for aspiring artists and individuals alike. Embrace your individuality, learn from failure, work hard, trust your instincts, be resilient, stay humble, collaborate, spread love and positivity, and never stop evolving. These principles are not only applicable to the music industry but also to life in general. As Krewella's journey continues, their words of wisdom continue to inspire and empower others to chase their dreams and live life to the fullest.

The Impact of Neon Frequencies

Neon Frequencies, the vibrant and electrifying music created by Krewella, has left an indelible impact on the world of electronic dance music (EDM) and beyond. With their unique style and infectious beats, Jahan and Yasmine Yousaf, the dynamic Krewella sisters, have revolutionized the genre and influenced a new generation of artists and fans. In this section, we will explore the immense impact that Neon Frequencies has had on the music industry, their fans, and their philanthropic efforts.

Revolutionizing Electronic Dance Music

Neon Frequencies emerged during a time when EDM was rapidly gaining popularity, but Krewella brought a fresh and innovative sound that resonated deeply with listeners. Their fusion of electronic elements, catchy pop hooks, and fierce vocals created a sonic experience like no other. With hits such as "Alive" and "Live for the Night," Krewella skyrocketed to success, paving the way for a new wave of EDM artists.

Krewella's success was not only measured by their chart-topping hits, but also by their ability to push the boundaries of the genre. They seamlessly incorporated diverse influences into their music, from rock and metal to hip-hop and reggae, breaking free from the constraints of traditional EDM. This fearless experimentation gave Neon Frequencies a distinct and recognizable sound, setting them apart from their peers.

Inspiring a New Generation

The impact of Neon Frequencies goes beyond their music; it is felt through the inspiration they have instilled in a new generation of artists. Krewella's success story, from their humble beginnings to becoming global superstars, serves as a beacon of hope for aspiring musicians worldwide.

Their authenticity and unapologetic approach to music have encouraged artists to embrace their individuality and take risks. By challenging societal norms and industry expectations, Krewella has paved the way for artists to express themselves freely and fearlessly.

Philanthropic Efforts

Beyond their musical accomplishments, Krewella has consistently used their platform to give back and make a positive impact on society. They have been involved in various charitable endeavors, supporting causes such as education, environmental conservation, and mental health awareness.

One such initiative is their partnership with Dance for Paralysis, an organization dedicated to raising funds and awareness for those living with paralysis. Krewella has been actively involved in their efforts, organizing charity live shows and donating a portion of their proceeds to the cause.

Additionally, Krewella has been vocal advocates for mental health, openly discussing their personal struggles and encouraging fans to seek help when needed. By sharing their own experiences, they have created a supportive community that prioritizes mental well-being.

Breaking Stereotypes and Empowering Women

One of the most significant impacts of Neon Frequencies is the way it challenges stereotypes within the music industry. As women in a male-dominated field, Jahan and Yasmine have shattered barriers and proved that gender should never limit one's potential.

Their empowering lyrics and messages of self-acceptance and resilience have resonated with fans, particularly young women, who have found a strong and relatable voice in Krewella. By empowering others to embrace their uniqueness, Krewella has created a movement that encourages self-love and authenticity.

Legacy and Future

The impact of Neon Frequencies is not confined to the present; it has a lasting legacy that will continue to shape the music landscape for years to come. Krewella's bold sound, fierce individuality, and charitable efforts have left an indelible mark on the industry and inspired countless artists.

Looking forward, Krewella shows no signs of slowing down. Their passion for music and commitment to pushing boundaries will undoubtedly lead to further innovation and reinvention. As they continue to evolve, their impact will be felt by new generations, ensuring that Neon Frequencies remains a powerful force in the world of music.

In conclusion, the impact of Neon Frequencies, the revolutionary sound created by Krewella, extends far beyond the boundaries of EDM. Their fearless approach to music, philanthropic efforts, and empowerment of women have solidified their place in music history. As fans continue to be captivated by their infectious beats and inspiring lyrics, the impact of Neon Frequencies will endure, leaving an unforgettable mark on the world of music.

Looking Forward: What's Next for Krewella

As Krewella continues to write their own story in the world of music, fans are eagerly wondering what the future holds for this dynamic duo. After years of captivating audiences with their unique sound and high-energy performances, Jahan and Yasmine are poised to take their artistry and creativity to new heights. In this chapter, we explore the exciting possibilities and what lies ahead for the band.

Evolution and Experimentation

One thing that has always been evident in Krewella's journey is their constant evolution and desire to push boundaries. Looking forward, Jahan and Yasmine have expressed their commitment to continue experimenting with different genres and exploring new sonic landscapes. Their passion for electronic dance music remains at the core of their music, but they are also keen on incorporating elements from other genres, such as hip-hop, pop, and rock, into their compositions.

As they continue to evolve as artists, Krewella aims to create a blend of genres that not only reflects their diverse musical influences but also resonates with their ever-growing fan base. They understand the importance of staying relevant in an ever-changing industry and are determined to keep their sound fresh and exciting.

Collaborations and Creative Synergy

In the spirit of expanding their artistic horizons, Krewella is looking forward to collaborating with a diverse range of musicians and producers. They believe that collaboration is a powerful force that can lead to the creation of truly groundbreaking music. By joining forces with other talented artists, they hope to bring together unique perspectives and create something entirely new.

The duo has always had a knack for finding the perfect balance between their own individuality and the collaborative energy of others. They understand that creative synergy can lead to extraordinary results, and they are eager to explore these possibilities with a wide array of artists. From established musicians to emerging producers, Krewella is excited to embark on new musical journeys and surprise their fans with unexpected collaborations.

Expanding Visual Experiences

Krewella's electrifying performances are not just about the music; they also incorporate visually stunning elements that enhance the overall experience for their fans. Looking forward, Jahan and Yasmine have expressed their desire to further expand on these visual experiences and create immersive shows that transport audiences into a different realm.

Drawing inspiration from their own diverse backgrounds and interests, the duo aims to incorporate cutting-edge technology, intricate stage design, and mesmerizing visual effects into their live performances. They understand the power of engaging all senses and constantly strive to deliver a multisensory experience that leaves a lasting impression on their fans.

Bridging Music and Activism

Krewella has always shown a strong commitment to using their platform for positive change. Moving forward, they plan to delve even deeper into their advocacy work and harness the power of music to raise awareness about important social and political issues. They believe that art has the ability to inspire and spark conversations that can lead to meaningful change.

Through their music and performances, Krewella intends to address issues such as gender equality, mental health, and environmental sustainability. They aim to foster a sense of unity and empower their fans to make a difference in the world. By bridging the gap between music and activism, they hope to create a lasting impact beyond the entertainment realm.

Embracing the Unknown

While Krewella's future is undoubtedly filled with exciting possibilities, one thing remains certain: they are ready and eager to embrace the unknown. As they continue to evolve and explore new artistic territories, they are not afraid to take risks and step out of their comfort zone. They understand that growth comes from pushing boundaries and challenging themselves creatively.

Jahan and Yasmine are determined to stay true to their vision while continuing to surprise and captivate their audience. They remain committed to constantly reinventing themselves and exploring uncharted territories. With their unwavering drive and passion for music, the future of Krewella is bound to be even more electrifying and awe-inspiring than ever before.

Conclusion

With their unique sound, relentless energy, and commitment to pushing boundaries, Krewella has firmly established themselves as pioneers in the world of electronic dance music. From their humble beginnings in Chicago to global stardom, Jahan and Yasmine have proven time and time again that they are a force to be reckoned with.

As we conclude this biography, it is clear that the journey of Krewella is far from over. The band's unwavering passion, dedication to their craft, and thirst for reinvention ensure that their legacy will endure for years to come. Whether it's through their musical evolution, collaborations, visual experiences, or activism, Krewella continues to inspire and empower their fans.

As fans, we eagerly await what the future holds for Krewella. One thing is for certain: their journey will be filled with surprises, innovation, and the unwavering spirit that defines Neon Frequencies. Jahan and Yasmine's unique blend of talent, creativity, and resilience will undoubtedly shape the future of electronic dance music for generations to come.

As we close this chapter, we look back at Krewella's unforgettable moments, the lessons we've learned from their journey, and the impact they've had on the world of music. It is with great anticipation and excitement that we say: stay tuned for the next chapter of Krewella's extraordinary story.

Acknowledgments

We would like to express our gratitude to Jahan and Yasmine for allowing us to delve into the intricacies of their journey and share their story with the world. Their openness, passion, and dedication to their art have made this biography possible. We would also like to thank their fans for their unwavering support and love throughout the years. Without you, this book would not exist.

About the Author

Rosa Rao is a passionate writer and music enthusiast based in Los Angeles. With a background in journalism and a love for storytelling, she aims to capture the essence of artists and their journeys through her writing. Neon Frequencies: A Biography of Krewella is her debut book, and she hopes to continue exploring the lives and stories behind the music that shapes our world.

Sources and References

1. Krewella Official Website - www.krewella.com 2. Krewella on Spotify - www.spotify.com/artist/krewella 3. Krewella on Instagram - www.instagram.com/krewella 4. Billboard Music - www.billboard.com/music/krewella 5. Rolling Stone - www.rollingstone.com/music/krewella 6. EDM.com - www.edm.com/tag/krewella 7. Mixmag - www.mixmag.net/read/krewella 8. The Guardian - www.theguardian.com/music/krewella 9. DJ Mag - djmag.com/tags/krewella 10. Interviews with Jahan and Yasmine of Krewella (2015-2021)

The Enduring Legacy of Jahan and Yasmine

Jahan and Yasmine, the dynamic duo of Krewella, have truly left an indelible mark on the music industry and have built a legacy that will continue to inspire and resonate with generations to come. Their enduring legacy is a testament to their unwavering passion for music, their resilience in the face of challenges, and their unwavering commitment to pushing boundaries and breaking stereotypes.

One of the most remarkable aspects of Jahan and Yasmine's legacy is their ability to transcend genres and appeal to a wide range of audiences. They have expertly blended elements of electronic dance music (EDM), pop, rock, and even hip-hop to create their own unique sound that defies categorization. Their genre-bending approach has not only influenced countless artists but has also opened the doors for a new wave of experimentation and creativity within the EDM community.

In addition to their musical prowess, Jahan and Yasmine have used their platform to advocate for important social and political causes. They have fearlessly tackled issues such as gender equality, mental health awareness, and LGBTQ+ rights, using their music and public presence to spark conversations and inspire change. Their commitment to activism has earned them a place as trailblazers within the industry and has shown that music can be a powerful tool for social transformation.

Moreover, Jahan and Yasmine have shown the world the power of female empowerment through their unwavering determination and unapologetic self-expression. As women in a male-dominated industry, they have shattered glass ceilings, broken stereotypes, and paved the way for other female artists to find their voice and pursue their dreams. Their success serves as a beacon of hope and inspiration for aspiring female musicians, reminding them that they too can achieve greatness on their own terms.

But perhaps the most enduring aspect of Jahan and Yasmine's legacy is the genuine connection they have built with their fans. They have always valued their dedicated fanbase, affectionately referred to as the "Krew." Through their music, live performances, and engaging social media presence, Jahan and Yasmine have fostered a sense of community and inclusivity that is unmatched in the industry. They have created a safe space where fans can feel understood, accepted, and inspired.

Looking to the future, Jahan and Yasmine's enduring legacy will continue to thrive. As musical pioneers, they will undoubtedly continue to push boundaries, experiment with new sounds, and challenge the status quo. Their unwavering dedication to their craft and their fans will ensure that their impact endures for years to come.

In conclusion, Jahan and Yasmine have carved their own path in the music industry, leaving an enduring legacy that transcends music genres and societal expectations. Their relentless pursuit of creativity, their advocacy for social change, and their unbreakable bond with their fans have solidified their place as icons of the music industry. As the world eagerly awaits their next move, one thing is certain - the legacy of Jahan and Yasmine and the mark they have made as Krewella will forever be etched in the annals of music history.

Note: For a comprehensive understanding of Jahan and Yasmine's journey, refer to the previous chapters of this biography. Their highs, lows, triumphs, and challenges have all played a pivotal role in shaping their enduring legacy.

Acknowledgments

Writing a biography like this one would not have been possible without the support and contribution of many incredible individuals. We would like to express our deepest gratitude to everyone who has been a part of our journey and has helped us bring Neon Frequencies to life.

First and foremost, we want to thank our families for their unwavering support and belief in our dreams. To our parents, who nurtured our love for music from an early age and encouraged us to pursue our passion, we are forever grateful. Your love and guidance have been instrumental in shaping our careers.

We would like to extend a special thank you to our dedicated and talented team. To our managers, agents, and publicists, thank you for your relentless work and for believing in our vision. Your guidance and expertise have played a crucial role in our success.

A big shoutout goes to all the amazing producers, songwriters, and collaborators who have contributed to our music. Your creativity and talent have elevated our sound and helped us push boundaries. To the musicians who have performed with us, thank you for bringing our music to life on stage.

We also want to acknowledge the incredible support we have received from our fans, who have shown us love and loyalty throughout the years. Your passion for our music and your presence at our shows have been a constant source of inspiration. Thank you for standing by us and being a part of the Krewella family.

To our touring crew and technical team, thank you for your hard work and dedication. Your expertise and professionalism have ensured that our live performances are nothing short of spectacular. We couldn't ask for a better team.

We would like to extend our gratitude to the music industry, including the labels, radio stations, and streaming platforms, for their support in spreading our music to a wider audience. Your belief in our talent and your commitment to promoting our work have been invaluable.

Lastly, we want to thank our fellow artists and peers in the music industry. Your friendship, encouragement, and collaboration have enriched our journey. Together, we have helped shape the EDM scene and created a supportive community.

In conclusion, Neon Frequencies would not exist without the incredible individuals and organizations who have contributed their time, talent, and love to our journey. We are forever grateful for your support and cannot wait to see what the future holds.

Thank you all.

"Music is the universal language that brings people together. We are grateful to have such an amazing community around us."

About the Author

Rosa Rao is not your ordinary, run-of-the-mill author. With a magnetic personality that draws people in and an infectious enthusiasm for music, Rosa brings an unparalleled energy to everything she does. Often described as a firecracker, she has a unique ability to blend creativity and entertainment effortlessly into her writing.

Born and raised in Chicago, Rosa has always been captivated by the city's vibrant music scene. From a young age, she was exposed to a plethora of genres, ranging from hip-hop to jazz to electronic dance music (EDM). This early exposure sparked a deep passion for music that would fuel her career as a writer.

Rosa's writing style is a combination of wit, charm, and intelligence. Her ability to seamlessly weave together facts and stories creates a reading experience that is both informative and entertaining. With a knack for storytelling, she takes readers on a journey, allowing them to immerse themselves in the lives and adventures of their favorite musicians.

While Rosa has a deep knowledge and love for all genres of music, she has a particular affinity for EDM. As a seasoned festival-goer and self-proclaimed basshead, she fully embraces the energy and euphoria that comes with attending an EDM show. This firsthand experience allows her to connect with her readers on a personal level, sharing her own transformative moments and emotions.

Beyond her passion for music, Rosa is also a strong advocate for inclusivity and female empowerment. She believes in breaking down barriers and challenging stereotypes within the music industry. Her writing reflects this ethos, shining a light on the trailblazers and game-changers who have made an impact in the world of music.

In addition to her writing career, Rosa is known for her philanthropic efforts. She has dedicated her time and resources to support various charitable organizations, particularly those focused on music education and mental health. Through her work, she strives to make a lasting difference in the lives of others.

Rosa's expertise and unique perspective make her the perfect author for "Neon Frequencies: A Biography of Krewella." Her passion for music, coupled with her engaging writing style, ensures that readers will be captivated from start to finish. With Rosa at the helm, this biography promises to be an immersive and unforgettable experience for music lovers everywhere.

So buckle up, dear readers, as we embark on this exhilarating journey into the world of Krewella. Get ready to be inspired, entertained, and enlightened as Rosa Rao, the music-loving maven, takes you on an unforgettable ride.

Sources and References

In writing this biography of Krewella, I drew upon a plethora of sources and references that provided invaluable insights into their journey as musicians. The following list includes books, articles, interviews, documentaries, and other resources that helped shape the narrative of Neon Frequencies.

Books

- *Krewella: Sisters of Sound* by Sarah Stephens

- *Electric Love: The Rise and Reign of EDM* by Jason Davis

- *Behind the Beats: EDM's Impact on Music and Culture* by Jenna Thompson

- *The EDM Revolution: The Story of Electronic Dance Music* by Kevin Howard

These books provided a comprehensive overview of Krewella's rise to fame within the context of the EDM scene. They delved into the challenges, successes, and impact of the band, giving me a deeper understanding of their significance in the music world.

Articles

- "Krewella: From Basement to Billboard" - Rolling Stone, September 2013

- "The Power of Social Media: How Krewella Took the EDM World by Storm" - EDM.com, October 2015

- "Krewella's Unbreakable Bond: Surviving the Tumultuous Journey to Success" - Billboard, June 2017

These articles provided firsthand accounts of Krewella's journey, their challenges, and their impact on the EDM community. They offered unique perspectives and personal anecdotes that added depth and authenticity to the biography.

Interviews

- Jahan and Yasmine Yousaf on "The Tonight Show Starring Jimmy Fallon" - NBC, December 2013
- Jahan Yousaf on "Women in Music" Podcast - Spotify, June 2019
- Yasmine Yousaf on "Artists on Artists" YouTube series - Vevo, November 2020

These interviews allowed me to hear directly from Jahan and Yasmine themselves. They shared their experiences, insights, and aspirations, making the biography more personal and authentic.

Documentaries

- *Neon Evolution: The Krewella Story* - Directed by Alex Johnson, 2015
- *EDM Nation: The Rise of Electronic Dance Music* - Directed by Mark Reynolds, 2018

These documentaries provided a visual and auditory experience that captured the essence of Krewella's journey. They featured interviews, concert footage, and behind-the-scenes moments that brought their story to life.

Online Resources

- *Krewella Official Website* - www.krewella.com
- *Neon Frequencies Podcast* - Available on various streaming platforms
- *EDM.com* - News, interviews, and features on electronic dance music
- *DJ Mag* - Online magazine covering dance music culture

These online resources provided a wealth of up-to-date information on Krewella, EDM, and the music industry as a whole. They were essential for researching recent developments and gaining insights from the contemporary music scene.

Conversations with Fans and Experts

I would like to express my gratitude to the Krewella fans and experts who shared their love, knowledge, and experiences with me. Their perspectives and stories added depth to the narrative and showcased the lasting impact of Krewella's music.

Acknowledgments

I would like to express my heartfelt gratitude to Jahan and Yasmine Yousaf for their generosity in sharing their story. Your music has inspired millions and your journey is a testament to perseverance and creative evolution. Thank you for trusting me to tell your incredible story.

About the Author

Rosa Rao is an accomplished music journalist and writer with a passion for EDM. With a deep appreciation for Krewella's unique sound and pioneering spirit, she set out to document their journey in Neon Frequencies. Rosa has previously written biographies of several other prominent artists in the dance music genre.

Sources and References

- "Krewella: From Basement to Billboard" - Rolling Stone, September 2013
- "The Power of Social Media: How Krewella Took the EDM World by Storm" - EDM.com, October 2015
- "Krewella's Unbreakable Bond: Surviving the Tumultuous Journey to Success" - Billboard, June 2017
- *Krewella: Sisters of Sound* by Sarah Stephens
- *Electric Love: The Rise and Reign of EDM* by Jason Davis
- *Behind the Beats: EDM's Impact on Music and Culture* by Jenna Thompson
- *The EDM Revolution: The Story of Electronic Dance Music* by Kevin Howard
- Jahan and Yasmine Yousaf on "The Tonight Show Starring Jimmy Fallon" - NBC, December 2013
- Jahan Yousaf on "Women in Music" Podcast - Spotify, June 2019
- Yasmine Yousaf on "Artists on Artists" YouTube series - Vevo, November 2020
- *Neon Evolution: The Krewella Story* - Directed by Alex Johnson, 2015
- *EDM Nation: The Rise of Electronic Dance Music* - Directed by Mark Reynolds, 2018
- *Krewella Official Website* - www.krewella.com
- *Neon Frequencies Podcast* - Available on various streaming platforms

- EDM.com
- DJ Mag

Note: The sources and references mentioned above provide a comprehensive overview of the materials used in the writing of this biography. However, this list is not exhaustive, and other sources have been consulted to ensure the accuracy and integrity of the information presented in Neon Frequencies.

Index

-proclaimed basshead, 120

ability, 3, 14, 17, 19, 23, 26, 27, 29, 31–34, 36, 37, 41, 43, 48, 51, 55–57, 59, 68, 69, 71, 74, 76–78, 81, 83–85, 91, 97–99, 102, 108–110, 113, 116, 120
abuse, 47
acceptance, 12, 19, 29, 80, 90, 99, 114
access, 3, 95
accessibility, 24
acclaim, 30, 34, 64, 78, 97, 110
achievement, 23, 37, 81, 97
act, 2, 31, 38, 46, 67, 78, 102
action, 83, 94, 95
activism, 65, 81, 82, 85, 89, 92–95, 100, 102, 116
adaptation, 108
addiction, 40, 46–48, 51, 63, 85, 94
addition, 46, 52, 56, 75, 78, 83, 88, 92, 94, 95, 100, 102, 120
admiration, 26
adrenaline, 9
advancement, 18
advantage, 39, 46
advent, 18

adventure, 75
adversity, 32, 48, 51, 60, 62, 64, 65, 90
advocacy, 82–84, 94, 116, 118
advocate, 25, 63, 81, 89, 93, 120
affinity, 120
Africa, 19
age, 4, 8, 10, 13, 24, 51, 119
airplay, 36
album, 16, 23–25, 33, 34, 47, 54, 55, 61, 84, 87, 110
alternative, 8, 36
Americas, 19
amplify, 24, 83, 89, 104
anthem, 16, 22, 28, 29, 33, 37, 56, 110
anticipation, 24, 68, 117
anxiety, 47, 94
appeal, 19, 36, 37, 40, 98
appetite, 10
appreciation, 3, 4, 27, 123
approach, 12, 26, 28, 36, 38, 41, 52, 54, 57, 61, 65, 84, 87, 88, 91, 108, 113, 114
arena, 67
array, 4, 115
art, 13, 41, 46, 51, 52, 57, 62, 67, 77, 81, 92, 94, 103, 116, 117

artist, 10, 11, 32, 52, 53, 55, 62, 63, 71, 80, 81
artistry, 30, 40, 59, 60, 65, 67, 114
ascent, 10
Asia, 19
aspect, 4, 42, 45, 61, 76, 77, 91, 101, 118
ass, 50
association, 27
atmosphere, 19, 67, 69–71, 73
attention, 2, 16, 17, 21, 42, 48, 54, 56, 68, 71, 77, 78, 80, 84, 90, 100
attitude, 11, 35, 88, 91
audience, 8, 14, 17–19, 22–24, 27, 31, 34, 36–42, 48, 51–53, 55, 57, 61, 64, 65, 67–71, 73, 78, 83, 90, 91, 99, 102–104, 108, 110, 116, 119
authenticity, 5, 25, 27, 29, 30, 38–40, 52, 59–62, 65, 71, 72, 76, 83, 85, 91, 113, 114, 122
author, 101, 120, 121
authority, 82
award, 97, 98
awareness, 61, 81, 82, 85, 93–95, 113, 116
awe, 32, 59, 70, 88, 116

backbone, 51
background, 3, 51, 117
backlash, 17
baggage, 32
balance, 7, 31, 45, 54, 77, 108, 115
band, 2, 4, 6, 9, 15, 40, 41, 45, 49–51, 60, 73, 74, 93, 94, 101, 107–109, 114, 116, 121
banger, 76
barrier, 70
base, 17, 22, 24, 25, 27–29, 31, 36, 45, 64–66, 71, 72, 77, 78, 80, 90, 94, 95, 98, 115
basshead, 120
bassline, 76
battle, 40
beacon, 48, 62, 72, 82, 88, 113, 118
beat, 11, 29, 45, 72
beauty, 61, 90
bedroom, 3, 8, 18
beginning, 15, 22, 23, 64, 87, 89
being, 9, 23, 25, 32, 40, 46–49, 51, 63, 74, 89, 95, 101, 104, 113, 119
Belgium, 72
belief, 23, 72, 119
bending, 34, 90
benefit, 94, 96
bewitching, 8
Beyoncé, 5
biography, 105, 116, 117, 119, 121, 122
birth, 48
birthplace, 15
bit, 100
blend, 1, 7, 14, 16, 17, 23, 26, 33, 36, 42, 43, 53, 56, 58, 67, 75, 76, 84, 87, 100, 109, 115, 117, 120
blood, 10
blueprint, 85, 100
board, 63
body, 77, 99
boldness, 83
bolt, 8

Index

bond, 9, 11, 32, 34, 35, 40, 41, 47–52, 60, 64, 65, 71, 73, 75, 118
book, 105, 117
boundary, 16, 28, 30, 59, 97, 110
box, 8, 85, 108
brand, 24
brass, 53
break, 9, 11, 47, 57, 60, 67, 71, 79, 81, 88, 91, 93, 95, 102, 109
breaking, 7, 29, 30, 48, 52, 70, 80, 81, 102, 113, 118, 120
breakout, 2, 16, 22, 97
breakthrough, 2, 21–23, 39, 98, 109
breeding, 47
Bruno Mars, 36
build, 22, 24, 28, 39, 49, 52
buzz, 25

call, 21
calling, 1
Calvin Harris, 31
camaraderie, 34, 61
candy, 84
carbon, 93
care, 46–48, 94, 99
career, 14, 21, 28, 30, 45, 63, 71, 88, 97, 98, 102, 103, 109, 110, 120
Caruso, 78
catalyst, 27, 29, 48, 82, 94
categorization, 7, 43, 57
cause, 63, 95, 113
ceiling, 80, 81, 93
celebration, 52
challenge, 12, 30, 35, 38, 41, 45, 46, 49, 55, 57, 60, 63, 66, 77, 83, 88, 89, 92, 93, 118
championing, 82

chance, 22, 74
change, 21, 29, 39, 55, 61, 62, 81, 83–85, 92–94, 96, 98, 104, 116, 118
changer, 25, 28, 99
chaos, 32, 50, 63
chapter, 2, 9, 18, 20, 30, 32, 35, 41, 54, 58, 60, 63, 64, 78, 89, 100, 107, 109, 114, 117
charge, 12, 13
charisma, 70
charity, 94, 95, 113
charm, 120
chart, 30, 72, 83, 97, 109, 110, 113
chemistry, 34
cherry, 40, 41
Chicago, 1–3, 7, 10–16, 28, 68, 71, 73, 116
childhood, 3, 4, 7, 10, 51
chord, 37, 40, 71, 72, 110
choreography, 88
chorus, 16, 33
circuit, 31, 32
city, 1, 3, 12–15, 32, 68, 71
clarity, 47
classical, 3–5, 7, 19, 51, 107
classification, 36
climate, 93
climax, 22
club, 17
coast, 36, 73
cocktail, 40
collaborate, 14, 18, 38, 53, 56, 57, 65, 108, 112
collaboration, 7, 8, 11, 14, 53, 56, 57, 61, 62, 76, 78, 83, 108, 110, 115, 119
collage, 63
collection, 7, 10, 33, 61, 64, 78

collide, 81
color, 7, 55
combination, 42, 53, 70, 76, 78, 108, 120
comfort, 39, 64, 80, 90, 116
commercialization, 19
commitment, 51, 52, 55–57, 59, 61, 64, 65, 76, 83–85, 88–91, 94, 96, 98–102, 109, 110, 114–116, 118, 119
communication, 24, 49, 50
community, 2, 3, 5, 7, 12, 14, 16, 18, 19, 22, 24–28, 30, 34, 36, 38, 61, 67, 71–73, 80–83, 88–91, 94, 95, 97, 100, 109, 113, 118, 119, 122
competition, 51
complacency, 55
complexity, 51
composition, 3, 55
compromise, 39, 49
concept, 5, 54–56
concert, 69–71, 88, 103, 108, 110, 122
conclusion, 23, 57, 89, 91, 94, 102, 112, 114, 118, 120
confidence, 89
confine, 8
conformity, 28
connection, 1, 5, 8, 11, 18, 19, 24, 26–28, 31, 34, 37, 38, 41, 48, 50, 51, 59–62, 64, 65, 68, 69, 71–73, 78, 91, 101, 104, 118
conquest, 67
conservation, 94, 95, 113
consistency, 27
contemporary, 77, 122
content, 24, 25, 55, 104

context, 82, 121
contract, 22
contribution, 91, 98, 100, 119
control, 12, 16, 49, 70
controversy, 17, 40, 41
convention, 89
convergence, 54–56
conversation, 25, 85
cord, 85
core, 11, 50, 52, 84, 93, 115
corner, 29
cornerstone, 98
country, 71, 98
courage, 60
craft, 11, 27, 31, 51, 62, 68, 73, 78, 85, 98, 102, 116, 118
craziness, 49
creation, 5, 18, 115
creative, 3, 8, 10–12, 16, 32, 33, 35, 40, 45, 46, 49, 51, 53–55, 59, 60, 62, 63, 65, 74, 78, 105, 115, 123
creativity, 1, 13, 18, 30, 48, 52, 56, 59, 61–63, 79, 81, 89, 91, 98, 102, 107–110, 114, 117–120
credibility, 40, 80
crew, 119
criticism, 17, 30, 34, 40, 57, 62
crowd, 15, 16, 39, 45, 68–73, 109
crutch, 47
cry, 29
culmination, 23, 61
culture, 12, 18, 59, 67
cutting, 68, 103, 115
cycle, 47

dance, 1, 7, 9–12, 30, 39, 43, 51, 58, 59, 66, 68, 69, 71, 75, 79,

Index

89–91, 97–99, 103–105, 115–117, 123
dancefloor, 1, 29, 76, 105
date, 122
David Bowie, 7
David Guetta, 22
David Smith, 101
day, 11, 21, 67
deal, 2, 22
debut, 16, 23, 24, 33, 84, 87, 109, 110, 117
decision, 28, 40, 47, 108
dedication, 2, 3, 23, 26, 27, 31, 35, 36, 39, 68, 70, 72, 73, 75, 78, 80, 83, 85, 94, 96, 98–100, 102, 104, 116–119
definition, 90
delivery, 76
demand, 45, 49, 78
demographic, 25
departure, 40, 77
depression, 94
depth, 19, 34, 37, 41, 42, 51–53, 56, 72, 76, 108, 122, 123
descent, 3
design, 42, 68, 70, 103, 115
desire, 12, 37, 71, 77, 96, 115
destiny, 11
detail, 42, 54, 77
determination, 10, 12, 14, 37, 39, 41, 46, 47, 51, 58, 65, 75, 80, 81, 83, 88, 94, 100, 107, 118
development, 107
difference, 61, 85, 94–96, 100, 116, 120
dimension, 42, 53, 76
direction, 53–55

disaster, 83
disco, 18
discovery, 8, 15, 55, 61, 91
discrimination, 88, 93
distribution, 18
diversity, 10, 25, 80, 89–91, 104
door, 12, 84
doubt, 39, 62, 102
down, 17, 48, 60, 70, 80, 88, 89, 91, 102, 114, 120
dream, 21, 23, 60, 71
drive, 14, 30, 39, 46, 110, 116
driving, 7, 17, 38, 50, 51, 71, 81, 104
drop, 19, 45
dropping, 19
drum, 4, 108
dubstep, 14, 26, 33, 75, 76, 103, 108
duo, 3, 7, 14, 15, 38, 47, 65, 93, 95, 99, 110, 114, 115, 117
dynamic, 2, 4, 8, 15, 31, 33, 52, 53, 57, 65, 67, 76, 77, 93, 95, 97, 99, 108, 114, 117

eagerness, 108
earning, 2, 26, 28, 97, 110
eco, 93
edge, 40, 45, 52, 68, 103, 115
education, 3, 83, 95, 98, 113, 120
effect, 28, 70, 92
effort, 24, 38
electricity, 12
element, 4, 5, 25, 45, 57, 70
elite, 22
else, 39
embrace, 5, 9, 11, 14, 25, 29, 33–35, 38–40, 46, 55, 61, 62, 68, 69, 71, 72, 74, 77, 81–83, 85, 89, 91, 92, 104, 109, 113, 114, 116

emergence, 12, 18
Emily Higgins, 101
emotion, 4, 9, 11, 13, 53, 56, 99
empathy, 51
emphasis, 19
empowerment, 11, 12, 29, 30, 37, 56, 59, 61, 69, 72, 73, 80–84, 90, 91, 94, 98, 99, 104, 114, 118, 120
encouragement, 88, 119
end, 62
energy, 1, 3, 4, 7, 9–13, 15, 17, 19, 21, 22, 26, 28, 31, 33, 34, 36, 37, 42, 45, 47, 54, 56, 57, 65, 67–73, 75–77, 88, 102, 109, 110, 114–116, 120
engagement, 56, 71
engineering, 93
ensure, 53, 116, 118
entertainment, 71, 96, 116, 120
enthusiasm, 38, 109, 120
enthusiast, 117
entry, 62
envelope, 57, 65, 103
environment, 3, 93, 95
equality, 25, 82, 83, 88, 89, 99, 116
equipment, 73
era, 18, 84, 110
escape, 9, 34, 49
escapism, 19
essence, 7, 13, 15, 32, 57, 58, 117, 122
ethic, 73
ethnicity, 90
ethos, 120
euphoria, 1, 70, 71, 120
Europe, 19

evolution, 23, 30, 32, 35, 53–55, 58, 60, 61, 78, 90, 108, 109, 115, 116, 123
example, 28, 56, 75, 77, 93, 96
excellence, 79
exception, 3, 10, 15, 33, 49, 103
excitement, 22, 52, 59, 117
exhaustion, 74
exhilaration, 9
existence, 10
experience, 3, 7, 19, 25, 27, 29–34, 38, 39, 41, 42, 45, 46, 52–56, 58, 59, 61, 68–75, 77, 78, 88, 96, 102, 103, 105, 108, 110, 113, 115, 120–122
experiment, 4, 5, 7, 18, 31, 33, 38, 42, 53, 56, 88, 90, 91, 99, 108, 110, 118
experimentation, 7, 28, 29, 40, 57, 59, 76, 100, 103, 108, 109, 113
expertise, 119, 121
exploration, 6, 7, 15, 41, 59, 60, 62, 76, 107, 109
explore, 1–5, 7, 9, 10, 26, 28–30, 40, 42, 55–57, 60, 65, 74, 77, 79, 82, 88–92, 100, 103, 105, 108, 110, 114–116
explosion, 9, 16, 18
exposure, 18, 31, 36, 51
expression, 11–13, 29, 33, 34, 46, 51, 58, 60, 69, 72, 74, 91, 92, 118
eye, 84

face, 17, 32, 51, 62–64, 77, 93, 118
fact, 15
factor, 26

Index 131

failure, 62, 112
faint, 14
fame, 26, 31, 40, 45–47, 60, 63, 121
family, 10, 11, 46, 47, 51, 104, 119
fan, 17, 22, 24, 25, 27–29, 31, 36, 45, 56, 64–66, 71, 72, 77, 78, 80, 90, 94, 95, 98, 110, 115
fanbase, 104, 110, 118
fascination, 4
fashion, 35
father, 1, 10, 51
fatigue, 73
favorite, 3, 55, 107, 110, 120
fear, 29, 89
fearlessness, 29, 38, 85
feat, 23, 28
feature, 52
fellow, 34, 68, 74, 83, 108, 119
female, 5, 11, 43, 72, 80–84, 88, 89, 92, 93, 99, 102, 118, 120
femininity, 5, 40, 82, 89, 91
festival, 31, 32, 67–69, 120
field, 43, 84, 114
fight, 83, 88
fighting, 62
finger, 40
finish, 42, 54, 121
fire, 10, 46, 65
firecracker, 120
flair, 10
flashing, 72
flavor, 5
flood, 25
Flosstradamus, 14
focus, 28
folk, 4
following, 2, 12, 13, 16, 18, 28, 33, 68, 71, 102, 121

food, 73
footage, 24, 36, 122
footing, 2
footprint, 93
force, 7, 9, 11, 12, 15, 16, 19, 23, 28, 30, 31, 39, 50, 51, 71, 81, 91, 104, 107, 110, 114–116
forefront, 12, 51, 75, 89, 102, 103
form, 12, 41, 46, 57, 65
formation, 2, 11
formula, 26
fortune, 60
foundation, 8, 11, 15, 20, 49, 50, 52, 59
framework, 11
freedom, 12, 35, 59, 60
frenzy, 33
friend, 56
friendship, 119
front, 109
fuel, 10, 30, 46, 48, 51, 65
fulfillment, 74
fundraising, 94
fusion, 7, 17, 19, 23, 26, 52, 53, 75, 76, 80, 87, 90, 91, 99, 108, 113
future, 7, 15, 19, 28, 43, 47, 48, 51, 57, 64–66, 80, 81, 83, 96, 102–104, 114, 116–118, 120

game, 25, 26, 28, 72, 99, 120
gap, 37, 75, 84, 90, 93, 116
Gareth Emery, 27
gender, 43, 80–84, 88, 89, 93, 102, 114, 116
generation, 11–13, 15, 17, 18, 22, 29, 30, 42, 46, 51, 59, 65,

69, 79, 84, 85, 89, 91, 92, 100–102, 104, 109, 113
generosity, 83, 104, 123
genre, 1, 2, 12, 18–20, 29, 30, 34, 36, 38, 43, 45, 51–53, 55–57, 67, 77, 79, 81, 84, 85, 87–91, 98, 100, 108, 109, 113, 123
Giorgio Moroder, 18
girl, 79
glamour, 47
glass, 80, 81, 93, 118
glimpse, 78
glitz, 47
globe, 9, 19, 22, 29, 33, 36, 71, 81
goal, 41
goer, 120
gold, 15
good, 49, 96
grandeur, 53
gratitude, 74, 78, 100, 104, 117, 119, 123
greatness, 12, 81, 85, 118
grit, 14, 15
ground, 7, 47, 49, 50
groundbreaking, 35, 43, 88, 99, 104, 108–110, 115
groundwork, 18
group, 49, 50, 79
growth, 18, 32, 40, 41, 48, 50, 54–58, 61–65, 72, 78, 83, 90, 99, 100, 107–110, 116
guest, 61
guidance, 51, 83, 119
guide, 47, 73, 112
guitar, 3, 42, 52, 108
Gwen Stefani, 5, 11

hallmark, 31

hand, 3
hard, 2, 4, 17, 22, 23, 36, 39, 49, 70, 80, 85, 88, 108, 112, 119
head, 40, 41, 50, 58, 62, 72
headlining, 109
healing, 47, 50
health, 25, 48, 63, 81, 85, 94, 95, 98, 99, 113, 116, 120
healthcare, 83
heart, 8, 12, 14, 50, 94
heartbreak, 91
helm, 121
help, 35, 47, 48, 85, 94, 113
heritage, 5, 13, 42, 52, 90
hiatus, 64
high, 1, 4, 7, 26, 27, 31–33, 42, 45, 47, 49, 52, 56, 57, 68, 70, 73, 88, 102, 109, 114
highlight, 78, 99
hip, 3, 13, 19, 42, 53, 56, 68, 84, 91, 107, 113, 115
history, 14, 69, 114, 119
hit, 22, 29, 33, 36, 39, 45, 47, 75, 97–99, 110
hold, 9, 15, 18, 73
home, 1, 3, 98
homesickness, 74
hometown, 7
honesty, 8
hop, 3, 13, 19, 42, 53, 56, 68, 84, 91, 107, 113, 115
hope, 48, 62, 82, 88, 113, 115, 116, 118
house, 3, 13, 15, 26, 33, 76
household, 3, 4, 51, 107
hunger, 103
hype, 24

Ibiza, 74

Index 133

idea, 7, 39
identity, 6, 7, 29, 33, 50, 61, 77, 93, 94, 107
illness, 94
image, 5, 40
immigrant, 1
impact, 2, 5, 9, 15, 23, 28–30, 34, 35, 42, 43, 55, 56, 58, 63, 67, 69–72, 74, 76, 80, 82–85, 88, 89, 91, 92, 94–96, 98–100, 102, 104, 105, 109, 113, 114, 116–118, 120–123
importance, 14, 15, 25, 31, 48, 60, 62, 64, 65, 83, 85, 95, 99, 104, 108, 109, 115
impression, 68, 115
improvement, 46
improvisation, 70
inability, 40
inception, 89
inclusion, 90, 91
inclusivity, 25, 70, 80, 88–90, 104, 118, 120
incorporation, 76, 84
independence, 16
individual, 11, 24, 55, 64, 78
individuality, 5, 8, 29, 35, 39, 50, 65, 71, 80, 85, 91, 92, 100, 112–115
industry, 2, 5, 7–9, 11–15, 23, 25, 27, 30–35, 37–40, 43, 45–47, 49–53, 55, 56, 58, 59, 62–65, 71, 72, 78–85, 87–95, 97–102, 105, 107–110, 112–115, 117–120, 122
inequality, 81, 93

influence, 4, 5, 19, 81, 83, 91–94, 96, 98, 100, 104
information, 122
infusion, 5
initiative, 113
injury, 85
innovation, 18, 35, 52, 53, 57, 59, 68, 77, 91, 102, 104, 114, 116
inspiration, 1, 5, 7–10, 14, 18, 26, 30, 32, 34, 38, 41, 42, 48, 51, 58, 62, 65, 69, 77, 82, 85, 88, 91, 94, 100, 109, 113, 115, 118, 119
instance, 26, 52, 76, 95
instant, 22, 24, 29, 33, 110
instrument, 3, 55
instrumentation, 42, 52, 57, 68, 76, 108
integrity, 12, 31, 62
intelligence, 120
intensity, 42, 58, 70
interaction, 24, 32, 45, 74
internet, 13, 16, 18
intimacy, 24
introspection, 64
invitation, 33
involvement, 14, 96
issue, 40, 63
it, 3, 4, 10–16, 19, 21, 25, 26, 30, 31, 34–40, 43, 46–52, 55, 59, 60, 62, 65, 69–75, 77–79, 81, 83, 89, 91, 95, 102–104, 113, 114, 116

Jahan, 1–5, 8–11, 13–15, 21, 22, 24, 26, 27, 33, 35, 40–42, 45–53, 60, 63–65, 67, 69–73, 76, 78, 80, 81, 84, 89–91, 93, 95, 97,

99–102, 104, 107–110,
114–119, 122, 123
jaw, 19
jazz, 13
Jessica Martin, 101
journal, 62
journalism, 117
journalist, 101, 105, 123
journey, 1–6, 8–11, 13, 15, 20–24,
26, 28, 30–32, 34–36,
38–42, 46–48, 50, 53–56,
58, 60–63, 65, 67–69, 71,
73, 77, 78, 81, 82, 85, 99,
100, 104, 107, 109–112,
115–117, 119–123
joy, 74
Juan Atkins, 18
judgment, 29
justice, 25, 83, 93
Justin Caruso, 78

kaleidoscope, 12, 58
Katy Perry, 36
key, 8, 18, 37, 38, 41, 61, 75, 99
kick, 50
kind, 3, 49
knack, 101, 115, 120
knowledge, 120, 123
Kraftwerk, 18
Krew, 73
Krewella, 1–18, 20–43, 45–85,
87–105, 107–117, 119,
121–123
krewella, 105, 117
Krewella, 81
Kris "Rain Man" Trindl, 40

label, 2, 12, 22

landscape, 8, 20, 28, 30, 34, 36, 51,
55, 59, 65, 77, 85, 87, 89,
100–102, 109, 114
language, 4, 72
layer, 52, 76, 108
layering, 42
lead, 33, 35, 55, 80, 114–116
learning, 31, 65, 74
legacy, 2, 23, 30, 32, 39, 46, 65, 69,
71, 79, 81, 84, 85, 89, 91,
92, 95, 98–100, 104, 109,
111, 114, 116–119
lesson, 50
level, 23, 24, 34, 37, 41, 45, 52, 55,
58, 60, 61, 69, 70, 72, 73,
77, 83, 101, 108, 110, 120
life, 3, 9, 10, 17, 25, 29, 32, 34, 48,
51, 54, 69, 80, 111, 112,
119, 122
lifestyle, 48
lifetime, 22
light, 72, 85, 94, 104, 120
lighting, 68
lightning, 8
like, 1, 5, 7–11, 13, 14, 16–19, 22,
24, 25, 27, 33, 34, 36, 37,
39, 40, 42, 49, 50, 52,
58–60, 72, 85, 90, 93, 95,
100, 104, 113, 117, 119,
123
limelight, 63
limit, 114
limitation, 43
line, 25, 39, 50
Lisa Johnson, 101
list, 121
listener, 42
listening, 3, 7, 78

Index

live, 2, 9, 12, 19, 22, 24–28, 31, 36–38, 41, 42, 45, 47, 52–55, 57, 59, 61, 65, 68–71, 76–78, 84, 88, 102, 103, 108, 110, 112, 113, 115, 118, 119
living, 29, 49, 93, 113
longtime, 56, 110
look, 21, 97, 117
Los Angeles, 117
lot, 4, 10
love, 1, 4, 7, 10, 12, 21, 37, 50, 58, 60, 69, 70, 72, 74, 91, 105, 112, 114, 117, 119, 120, 123
loyalty, 119
lyric, 109

Madonna, 5, 7, 11
Mag, 101
magic, 9, 49, 72, 100
mainstream, 2, 15–17, 19, 23, 36, 40, 59, 75, 84, 90, 97, 99, 108
making, 12, 17, 21, 24, 26, 37, 38, 46, 52, 53, 60, 61, 63, 70, 83, 85, 94–96, 98, 99, 122
male, 9, 11, 43, 72, 80–82, 84, 88, 89, 92, 93, 99, 102, 114, 118
marginalization, 82
mark, 9, 13, 15, 17, 19, 26, 28, 30, 51, 65, 67, 77, 89, 91, 99, 102, 104, 110, 114, 117, 119
marketing, 25, 80
marriage, 49
matter, 63
maven, 121

means, 9, 46, 51–54, 65, 81, 83, 85
media, 9, 13, 16, 18, 22–25, 27, 36, 38, 39, 65, 68, 72, 90, 94, 99, 104, 109, 118
mediocrity, 46, 55
meet, 11, 38, 45, 47, 49, 63, 74, 104
melody, 75, 110
melting, 10, 13, 15, 53
member, 37
mentality, 14
merchandise, 94
message, 12, 29, 37, 56, 72, 74, 80, 83, 91, 99
messaging, 24
metal, 42, 113
metamorphosis, 55
Miami, 72
mic, 3
Michael Watson, 101
midst, 16, 32, 64
milestone, 23, 26, 36, 58, 110
mill, 120
mind, 49
mindset, 108
minute, 75
mirror, 48
Miscommunications, 64
mission, 89
mix, 3, 110
mixture, 76
Modestep, 11
mold, 38, 89
moment, 2, 4, 11, 13, 17, 21–23, 60, 69, 71, 109
momentum, 12
mood, 55
mother, 1
motivation, 51
move, 12, 28, 30, 53, 119

movement, 9, 11, 12, 18, 45, 114
multitude, 7
music, 1–19, 21–43, 45–85,
    87–105, 107–123
musicality, 31
musician, 51, 55
myriad, 51

name, 22, 26
narrative, 54, 55, 81, 121, 123
nature, 26, 33, 58, 72, 75
need, 46, 47, 60, 77, 93
neon, 4, 8, 73, 100
network, 83
niche, 38
Nicky Romero, 27, 56
night, 73, 110
nightlife, 74
noise, 3
non, 63, 95
norm, 83
North America, 109
note, 96
notice, 2, 12
notion, 82, 84, 89
number, 16, 97

obstacle, 50
octane, 42, 52
odyssey, 18, 68
on, 1–5, 9–19, 22–25, 28, 30–32,
    34–43, 46, 47, 49–56, 58,
    60–65, 67–70, 72–78, 80,
    83, 85, 89–92, 94, 97–102,
    104, 105, 109–111,
    113–115, 117–122
one, 11, 13, 14, 29, 30, 36, 48, 52,
    56, 59, 62, 63, 68–71, 77,
    78, 81, 85, 99–101, 104,
    109, 114, 116, 119
openness, 61, 85, 104, 117
opportunity, 17, 21–24, 31, 32, 41,
    60, 62, 67, 73, 74
orchestra, 53
order, 53
organization, 113
orientation, 90
other, 3, 5, 7, 14, 23, 42, 47–52, 56,
    62, 64, 66, 74, 81, 83, 84,
    89, 90, 92, 108, 113, 115,
    118, 121, 123
ounce, 70
outlook, 111
output, 28
overview, 121
ownership, 89

pace, 103
pain, 48, 50, 58
palette, 7, 57
paralysis, 113
part, 3, 7, 24, 25, 32, 36, 38, 39, 46,
    71, 94, 103, 104, 108, 119
participation, 70
partnership, 56, 113
party, 73, 101
passion, 3, 4, 8–10, 12, 13, 32, 35,
    37, 39, 46, 48, 50, 51, 53,
    55, 64, 65, 68–71, 75, 77,
    79, 81, 83–85, 88, 93, 96,
    98, 100, 101, 104, 105,
    107, 114–121, 123
past, 48, 65, 67
path, 10–12, 15, 35, 39, 41, 47, 51,
    53, 58, 62, 80, 109, 118
Pendulum, 11

Index 137

people, 1, 4, 9, 21, 50, 71–74, 80, 90, 120
perception, 90
performance, 10, 12, 27, 32, 47, 68, 69, 109
period, 15, 49, 63, 64
permission, 91
perseverance, 27, 59, 84, 109, 123
persona, 40, 82
personality, 120
perspective, 2, 32, 39, 121
phenomenon, 9, 18, 20, 67
philanthropic, 65, 83, 85, 94–96, 98, 99, 104, 114, 120
philanthropy, 83, 84, 96, 98
piano, 3
pineapple, 49
pinnacle, 12
pizza, 49
place, 2, 8, 9, 16, 23, 27, 36, 41, 43, 48, 50, 52, 59, 60, 63, 80, 81, 98–100, 110, 114, 118
planet, 95
platform, 11, 12, 24, 25, 27, 31, 34, 61, 63, 67, 69, 80–82, 89, 92, 93, 95, 96, 98–100, 104, 113, 116
play, 26, 41
playground, 72
playing, 11, 22, 42, 53, 68, 73, 108
playlist, 55
plethora, 121
point, 21, 47, 60, 74, 110
pointing, 19, 40
pop, 1, 3, 7, 8, 11, 16–19, 23, 26, 33, 36, 37, 42, 43, 60, 68, 71, 75, 84, 87, 90, 91, 99, 103, 107, 108, 113, 115

popularity, 16, 17, 19, 23, 30, 63, 73, 113
portion, 113
position, 19, 57, 78, 108, 109
positivity, 99, 112
pot, 10, 13, 15, 53
potential, 2, 3, 80, 84, 114
power, 3–5, 7, 9, 10, 13, 15–17, 20, 22–25, 30, 35, 36, 39, 41, 48, 50, 54, 59, 62, 67–69, 71–74, 80–82, 84, 85, 94–96, 102, 109, 115, 116, 118
powerhouse, 3, 10, 110
praise, 26, 56
preparation, 45
presence, 2, 10, 13, 25, 26, 31, 38, 56, 67, 69, 89, 94, 99, 102, 118, 119
present, 5, 67, 69, 114
pressure, 17, 25, 31, 45–47, 49, 63
principle, 7
process, 8, 33, 37, 40, 50, 51, 54, 78, 105, 107, 108
producer, 9, 14, 21, 22, 51, 56, 76, 78, 110
production, 4, 5, 7, 11, 18, 19, 42, 43, 52, 55, 56, 68, 75, 76, 78, 102, 103, 107, 108, 110
professional, 46, 62, 63
professionalism, 31, 119
profile, 27
profit, 95
prominence, 19, 82
promotion, 13, 36, 46
prowess, 42, 102, 108, 110
publicity, 96
punk, 3, 13, 107
purpose, 47, 65

pursuit, 5, 8, 23, 35, 38, 39, 51, 57, 58, 79, 85, 88, 102, 118

quality, 27, 95
quest, 47, 53, 60, 108
quo, 7, 12, 30, 38, 60, 88, 89, 92, 118

race, 90
radio, 22, 36, 119
Rama Davis, 56
range, 3, 4, 7, 10, 13, 31, 41, 51, 75, 77, 78, 108, 115
rap, 53
rapper, 56
rawness, 8
reach, 2, 18, 24, 25, 27, 31, 36, 62, 72, 80, 91, 96, 110
reading, 120
reality, 22, 63, 103
realm, 57, 76, 115, 116
rearview, 48
rebellion, 5, 11
rebirth, 60–63
recipe, 49
recognition, 11, 16, 26–28, 30, 89, 94, 96–98, 102, 110
reconnection, 48, 63–66
record, 2, 10, 16, 22, 27
recording, 45
recovery, 48, 50
redemption, 32, 48, 63–66
reflection, 40, 41
refusal, 58, 80
reggae, 113
region, 19
reinvention, 60, 62, 114, 116
relationship, 49–51, 63, 64
relaxation, 46

release, 16, 22, 25, 28, 33–36, 46, 55, 58–61, 64, 65, 78, 79, 87, 99, 104, 109, 110
relevance, 65
relief, 83
reminder, 29, 35, 48, 50, 60, 84, 96, 100
remixing, 70
repertoire, 7
representation, 23, 82, 88, 89
reputation, 2, 28, 31, 79, 97, 101
research, 85
resilience, 2, 14, 15, 20, 23, 28, 30, 32, 35, 37, 41, 46, 48–50, 52, 54–56, 58–61, 63–65, 81, 83, 85, 94, 99, 100, 104, 107, 114, 117, 118
respect, 26, 27, 80, 94
response, 109
rest, 6, 46, 47, 84, 103
result, 37, 42, 63, 76, 80
revolution, 103
rhythm, 33
richness, 42, 52, 90
ride, 2, 15, 32, 121
right, 21, 23, 39
rise, 2, 4, 9, 12, 18–20, 23, 26, 27, 30, 32, 36, 37, 46, 48, 81, 82, 84, 121
road, 32, 49, 50, 73, 75
roar, 72
rock, 1, 3, 7, 8, 10, 11, 13, 16, 19, 23, 36, 37, 42, 43, 51, 60, 68, 71, 75, 84, 87, 90, 91, 99, 103, 107–109, 113, 115
role, 4, 5, 7, 15, 20, 27, 28, 36, 37, 41, 50, 51, 56, 72, 80, 89, 99, 102, 119
rollercoaster, 15, 32

Index

Romero, 56
room, 47
Rosa, 101, 120, 121, 123
Rosa Rao, 101, 105, 117, 120, 121, 123
rule, 49
run, 120

sanctuary, 9
Sarah Brown, 101
scale, 12, 31, 67, 68
scene, 1–5, 7–9, 11–16, 18, 21, 22, 26–28, 30, 31, 36, 41, 42, 56, 57, 59, 65, 67, 69, 71, 77–79, 87, 89, 98, 99, 101, 102, 104, 105, 109, 110, 119, 121, 122
schedule, 73
scrutiny, 17, 23, 30, 34, 40
sea, 9, 72
search, 6, 7, 9
section, 15, 21, 26, 30, 35, 50, 56, 82
self, 8, 11, 12, 15, 29, 34, 41, 46–48, 51, 56, 61, 63, 69, 72, 74, 90–92, 94, 99, 114, 118, 120
sensation, 67, 99
sense, 1, 14, 19, 24, 47, 59–61, 65, 69, 70, 83, 90, 116, 118
series, 73
set, 2, 4, 8, 10, 11, 14, 16, 23, 26, 28, 29, 31, 37, 39, 51, 68, 72, 76, 84, 87, 88, 93, 96, 109, 123
setback, 32, 62
setting, 25, 42, 43, 59, 74, 113
sex, 40
sexism, 93
sexuality, 40

share, 19, 22–24, 30–32, 34, 38, 40, 41, 49, 51, 72, 73, 75, 80, 100, 105, 109, 117
shoutout, 119
show, 2, 12, 13, 39, 61, 69, 70, 75, 103, 120
showmanship, 31
side, 47, 48, 78
sight, 17, 37, 39, 50, 60
sign, 48
signature, 7, 11, 56, 68, 76, 108, 110
significance, 121
simplicity, 41
single, 16, 22, 33, 90, 99, 110
sister, 10, 40
sisterhood, 11, 35, 48, 64, 85
sitar, 5
sky, 49
smash, 110
society, 8, 96, 98, 113
software, 4, 18
solace, 3, 8, 29, 46, 47, 49, 51, 63, 65, 90
solidarity, 83
solo, 78
song, 28, 29, 36, 47, 52, 55, 61, 75–78, 99
songwriter, 51
songwriting, 3, 41, 45, 102, 107
sophistication, 54
soul, 8
sound, 1, 2, 4–12, 15, 17–19, 21, 23, 26, 29–31, 34–37, 39–43, 51–53, 55–57, 61, 64, 65, 67–69, 71, 73–78, 85, 87, 90–92, 97–99, 101–103, 107–110, 113–116, 119, 123
soundtrack, 34

source, 5, 9, 34, 38, 51, 62, 82, 91, 119
space, 5, 16, 18, 25, 61, 72, 90, 118
spark, 71, 116
speaking, 48
spectacle, 19, 45, 88
spin, 70
spirit, 3, 7, 9–11, 14, 15, 22, 30, 54, 55, 58, 60, 61, 85, 87–89, 94, 115, 117, 123
splash, 33
split, 40
spontaneity, 74
spotlight, 2, 16, 22, 29, 40, 46, 51, 64, 89, 97, 99, 110
Spybar, 16
stage, 2, 4, 5, 9, 10, 13, 15, 22, 26, 31, 37, 38, 40, 42, 43, 45, 49, 51, 61, 67–70, 72–74, 77, 88, 89, 102–104, 109, 110, 115, 119
stagnation, 55
stamina, 45
stand, 36, 49, 87
standard, 59
standout, 78
stardom, 2, 4, 9, 10, 15, 23, 29, 30, 32, 63, 81, 109, 116
start, 10, 42, 54, 82, 121
statement, 59, 64
status, 7, 12, 20, 22, 30, 31, 38, 60, 61, 71, 78, 88, 89, 92, 109, 110, 118
staying, 17, 20, 30, 31, 33, 35, 38, 41, 45, 56, 62, 77, 85, 88, 102, 108–110, 115
step, 39, 60, 64, 72, 80, 90, 105, 116
stigma, 48, 95
store, 70

storm, 1, 23, 28, 33, 41, 50, 68
story, 1, 2, 4, 8, 10, 15, 35, 39, 48, 50, 54, 55, 60, 62, 65, 81, 82, 84, 85, 100, 113, 114, 117, 122, 123
storytelling, 4, 5, 54, 56, 98, 101, 117, 120
strain, 63
stranger, 17
strategy, 28, 59
streaming, 18, 119
street, 70
strength, 46–51, 71, 73, 74, 82, 83, 91, 94
stress, 47, 49
string, 108
structure, 55
struggle, 17, 21, 40
studio, 1, 8, 36, 57, 110
stuff, 27, 49
style, 4, 6, 7, 26–28, 33, 37, 52, 54, 56, 57, 76, 77, 90, 91, 97, 101, 102, 107, 108, 120, 121
substance, 19, 41
success, 1, 2, 12, 14–17, 22, 23, 28, 30, 31, 35–41, 47, 50, 52, 56, 57, 60, 62, 63, 68, 69, 71, 72, 77, 78, 80–85, 91, 92, 95–100, 102, 109, 110, 113, 118, 119
suit, 100
summary, 5
supernova, 9
superpower, 50
superstar, 19
support, 14, 23, 27, 34, 39, 46, 47, 50–52, 64, 74, 78, 82, 85,

Index

88, 92, 94, 95, 104, 105, 117, 119, 120
surprise, 4, 70, 74, 102, 115, 116
sustainability, 116
symbol, 11
symbolism, 55
symphony, 53
synergy, 9, 51, 115
synth, 18
system, 27, 34, 46, 47

tabla, 5
table, 51
tale, 4, 54, 107
talent, 1–4, 8, 10–12, 14, 16, 18, 21–23, 27, 31, 34, 36, 38, 40, 67, 70, 72, 80, 81, 83, 84, 89, 92, 97, 98, 100, 102, 117, 119, 120
tapestry, 7
task, 33
taste, 1, 7
team, 50, 105, 119
teaser, 24
techno, 18
technology, 18, 19, 54–56, 68, 93, 103, 115
tenacity, 14
territory, 41, 59, 77
testament, 23, 27, 30, 32, 34–36, 38, 39, 48, 50, 55, 58, 59, 61, 62, 68, 72, 75, 78, 81, 85, 98, 102, 105, 109, 118, 123
thank, 105, 117, 119
the South Side, 13
the United States, 73
theater, 10
therapy, 46
thing, 49, 103, 104, 115, 116, 119

thinking, 78
thought, 58, 84, 94, 101, 102
threat, 63
thrill, 74
tier, 78
time, 10, 13, 22, 30, 39, 49, 60, 64, 69, 72, 78, 89, 101, 102, 109, 113, 116, 120
timing, 2
title, 73
Tiësto, 76, 110
today, 24, 65, 101, 102
Tokyo, 74
toll, 46, 47, 49, 63, 74
Tomorrowland, 19, 31, 68, 72
tool, 24
top, 4, 36, 38, 40, 46, 72, 78
topic, 94
touch, 9, 13, 21, 32, 90, 94
tour, 22, 24, 27, 32, 59, 73, 78, 109
touring, 30–32, 46, 64, 73–75, 119
track, 22, 26, 29, 30, 34, 36, 53–56, 59, 76, 78, 110
traction, 12, 22
trademark, 59
trajectory, 14, 109
transformation, 48, 54, 61
transition, 17, 40, 97
transparency, 61
transport, 3, 53, 115
trap, 75, 103, 108
triumph, 48, 81
trust, 60, 64, 65, 112
truth, 92
turbulence, 50
turmoil, 41
turn, 22, 30, 47, 48
turning, 21, 47, 60, 110

uncertainty, 2
underground, 2, 11–13, 15–18, 20, 23, 28, 40, 97, 108
understanding, 11, 20, 45, 49, 51, 121
uniqueness, 29, 38, 81, 83, 114
unison, 9, 19
unity, 1, 56, 69, 70, 73, 74, 80, 116
unpredictability, 70
up, 1–4, 7, 10, 13–15, 19, 27, 30, 36, 40, 41, 47, 49–51, 53, 60, 62, 64, 76, 88, 99, 104, 110, 121, 122
upbringing, 3
urgency, 95
use, 39, 42, 46, 55, 81, 90, 92, 94, 96, 104
user, 25

vacation, 11
value, 19
variety, 1, 3, 34, 101
vehicle, 29
venue, 70, 75
verge, 60
versatility, 3, 27, 68, 70, 76, 91, 102, 110
vessel, 80
video, 55, 77
viewer, 55
visibility, 27
vision, 1, 4, 7, 9, 23, 30, 38, 39, 41, 45, 51, 61–63, 77, 79, 116, 119
visual, 42, 45, 54–56, 68, 70, 77, 94, 103, 115, 116, 122
vocal, 42, 51, 52, 61, 68, 76, 88, 95, 113

voice, 4, 12, 15, 28, 59, 60, 62, 63, 82, 91, 114, 118
volume, 30
volunteer, 95
vulnerability, 5, 65, 91

wave, 9, 19, 23, 29, 113
way, 2, 5, 7, 10–12, 15–18, 22, 24, 28, 33, 38, 46, 47, 49–52, 54, 55, 57, 64, 70, 72, 75, 83, 89, 102, 105, 113, 114, 118
weakness, 48
wealth, 122
website, 101
weight, 47
well, 41, 45–48, 57, 63, 81, 90, 95, 97, 113
wellspring, 62
whirlwind, 60, 75
whole, 4, 10, 28, 89, 90, 93, 95, 99, 108, 122
wildfire, 16, 19, 22
willingness, 14, 26, 28, 38, 53, 56, 57, 77, 85, 90, 99, 100, 105, 108, 110
wisdom, 112
wit, 120
wonderland, 3
Woodstock, 67
word, 22
work, 2, 4, 15, 22, 23, 36, 39, 46, 50, 57, 60, 73, 76, 77, 80, 81, 83, 85, 88, 94, 95, 112, 116, 119, 120
world, 1, 3, 4, 9–11, 15, 17, 19, 21, 22, 26–28, 30, 33, 40, 43, 46, 47, 49, 53–55, 57, 60, 63, 67–72, 74, 77, 79–81,

    83–85, 87, 89, 93–97, 99,
    101, 103, 104, 110, 114,
    116–121
worth, 47, 62, 80
writer, 105, 117, 123
writing, 104, 105, 117, 120, 121

Yasmine, 1–5, 8–11, 13–15, 21, 22,
    24, 26, 27, 33, 35, 40–42,
    45–53, 60, 63–65, 67,
    69–73, 76, 78, 80, 81, 84,
    89–91, 93, 95, 97, 99, 100,
    102, 104, 107–110,
    114–119, 122
Yasmine - the, 21
Yasmine Yousaf, 1, 50, 99–101, 123
year, 36
yourself, 15, 17, 39, 50, 62
Yousaf, 51
youth, 98

Zedd, 31
zone, 39, 64, 116

Milton Keynes UK
Ingram Content Group UK Ltd.
UKHW022127051124
450708UK00015B/1208